2 -

Crazy Patchwork

Meryl Potter

Lothian
B O O K S

Dedication

To Trundles, Chief, Geeny, Wheels,
Yo, Castoff, Katie Pi and TM

Special thanks to
Jan Düttmer who, as always,
has created wonderful illustrations.

Thomas C. Lothian Pty Ltd
11 Munro Street, Port Melbourne, Victoria 3207

Copyright © text and illustrations Meryl Potter 1997
First published 1997
Reprinted 1998

National Library of Australia
Cataloguing-in-Publication data:

Potter, Meryl.

   Crazy patchwork.

   Bibliography.
   Includes index.
   ISBN 0 85091 797 2.

   1. Patchwork — Patterns. I. Title. (Series: Lothian
   craft series).

746.46041

Cover and text design by Jo Waite Design
All projects by Meryl Potter
Photographs by Rodney Weidland
Illustrations by Jan Düttmer
Printed in Singapore by Kin Keong Printing Co. Pte Ltd

US terms and metric conversions

Stranded embroidery cotton = floss
Stranded silk thread = silk floss
Calico = muslin or homespun
Paper: where A4 is required, use a sheet of foolscap
paper; A3 paper is twice the size of A4, so use a sheet
of drawing paper or join two pieces of foolscap, or
use pattern paper.

Fabric widths and yardages

90 cm wide fabric = 36 inches
110 cm wide fabric = 44 inches
1 metre = 40 inches
Generous yardages are given throughout, so where 1
or 2 metres are needed, simply buy 1 or 2 yards; for 3
metres, buy $3\frac{1}{3}$ yards. For 25 cm of fabric buy $\frac{1}{4}$ yard;
for 30, 40 or 50 centimetres, buy $\frac{1}{2}$ yard; for 60 cm
buy $\frac{3}{4}$ yard; for 1.2 metres buy $1\frac{1}{3}$ or $1\frac{1}{2}$ yards.

Measurements

Metric measurements do not convert into simple
imperial measurements. The simplest way of following instructions in the book is to use a metric ruler
(Omnigrid make a metric quilter's ruler) and tape
measure. You don't have to make any calculations in
this book so you don't need to understand the metric
system to make the projects — just use the measurements on the ruler. If you want to use imperial measures, a short list of approximate conversions follows.
Where you need to cut strips of fabric to match a pattern (for instance, for the Victorian purse), just
remove a tiny amount from each edge of the pattern
to give you an easy inch measurement to work with.
For most patterns the size will not matter. For the
calico (muslin) and Pellon base pieces, round up to
the nearest easy-to-use inch measurement: accuracy
doesn't matter here. To cut strips of fabric for double
binding, multiply the desired finished size by six.

For a quick conversion, divide the metric measurements by 2.5 to see the rough inch equivalent.

Seam allowances

0.5 cm (5 mm): use $\frac{1}{4}$ inch
1 cm: use $\frac{1}{2}$ inch
(These are both a little more than the metric equiva-
lents but that won't make a lot of difference to the
finished size.)

Approximate conversions to use with common measurements in this book (multiples of 5 are the closest conversions)

1.5 cm = $\frac{5}{8}$ inch	18 cm = $7\frac{1}{4}$ inches
2.5 cm = 1 inch	20 cm = 8 inches
5 cm = 2 inches	21 cm = $8\frac{1}{2}$ inches
6 cm = $2\frac{1}{2}$ inches	25 cm = 10 inches
10 cm = 4 inches	30 cm = 12 inches
12 cm = 5 inches	35 cm = 14 inches
14 cm = $5\frac{1}{2}$ inches	40 cm = 16 inches
15 cm = 6 inches	50 cm = 20 inches
16 cm = $6\frac{1}{2}$ inches	60 cm = 24 inches

CONTENTS

Crazy from the start

A CRAZE AT THE END of the nineteenth century — in America, England and Australia — crazy patchwork has been enjoying a quiet revival in recent years. Crazy patchwork is made up of odd-shaped scraps of fabric entirely covering a foundation fabric. The entire surface is then decorated with embroidery — as much or as little as you want.

Originally, each scrap, with its raw edge turned under, was set on the foundation fabric and stitched in place with a line of embroidery. All kinds of fancy fabrics were used — silks, brocades and velvets, as well as embroidered fabrics, ribbons and braids. And while some stitchers confined themselves to feather and herringbone stitches, others seem to have used every stitch they knew, and added simple or elaborate embroidered motifs in larger spaces.

Today, the pleasure that crazy patchwork offered nineteenth-century stitchers — collecting pieces of beautiful fabrics, or finding a use for precious or sentimental scraps from the workbasket, and showing off embroidery skills — still has great appeal. And although we now stitch the fabrics in place with a sewing machine, we still embroider every seam. For patchworkers who want to include embroidery in their quilts, and for embroiderers who want to try patchwork, crazy patchwork is the answer.

The nineteenth-century crazy patchworker made large coverlets for the bed as well as smaller pieces, such as teacosies and cushions, to decorate the house. In this book, you will find a coverlet, if you want to try a large project, and plenty of small practical projects, including boxes and a cushion, as well as quick pieces such as brooches, sachets and pincushions.

As you like it

One of the greatest joys of doing crazy patchwork is its spontaneity. There are no graphs to follow stitch by stitch, and no detailed patterns to transfer meticulously onto your fabric. You won't need to buy lots of new threads in specific colours, or six metres of new fabric for every project: crazy patchwork will use whatever is lurking in the bottom of the cupboard.

You *can* plan the placement and shape of every piece of fabric, and you *can* plot the use of stitches and the placement of embroidered motifs — but you don't have to! Once you have chosen your colour scheme, you can simply sit down at the sewing machine and let 'er rip. Selecting fabrics from your stash as you go, cutting, shaping and stitching each piece as you add it, is all you need to do.

And when it comes to the embroidery, you can emulate your nineteenth-century sisters and restrict yourself to just one or two stitches, or you can throw every stitch you know onto the surface of your patchwork. As for larger motifs, all of those included in this book require only the simplest lines to guide them, and none of them needs to be traced. But if you want to include Kate Greenaway children, as the Victorian embroiderers did, or richly detailed satin stitch flowers, you can do that too. You can make your crazy patchwork as restrained or as luxuriant as you like — there really aren't any rules to follow.

This book includes diagrams showing you how to work a variety of favourite crazy stitches, and plenty of ideas for how to use them and how to combine them (the *Index* on page 72 gives the location of all stitches in the book). Making stacks of stitches, all sitting above each other in rows, can be a good way of filling large spaces without having to think up a motif. Simple motifs to suit the theme of each piece, whether underwater creatures or stars, are also included.

Patterns and detailed step-by-step instructions tell you how to make up each piece. However, you won't find patterns that you have to follow for piecing the crazy patchwork itself — it is impossible to reproduce precisely a patchwork base: your fabrics will be different weights, sizes, shapes, colours and patterns from the ones I have used (and your tastes will be different).

As for the thread to use, the number of strands, the type and size of needle, these should be chosen to suit your fabrics and the size of the finished piece. If you make in brocades and heavy silks or cottons what I have made in Thai silk, using a single strand of stranded silk thread and a number 10 crewel needle will not work at all — your embroidery will disappear. There is plenty of advice in *Techniques and technicalities* (pages 63–9) about threads, needles and so on, so follow that if you feel uncertain.

You may wish to make projects in the same colours as the ones in this book, but you don't have to — every one of them can be made in your own colour scheme and fabrics. You don't have to put sea motifs with sea colours, and if you want to put sea motifs on your red and green Christmas decorations, you can do that too.

Your crazy patchwork will use *your* hoard of threads and fabrics, and the instructions have been written with that in mind.

Above all, crazy patchwork is fun, and it offers stitchers infinite possibilities, by using all kinds of fabrics, ribbons, laces, threads, stitches and three-dimensional treasures. Whether you stick to your all-time favourites, and show off all the things you do best, or try new techniques, or are just beginning to try patchwork or embroidery, crazy patchwork is for you.

The Stitch Police

We all seem to have friends or relatives who tell us that their grandmother did beautiful embroidery, or that Great Aunty Myrtle's work was so exquisite that it was displayed back to front at the local show! The implication is that, somehow, your work just doesn't measure up. I call these people the Stitch Police, as they are always ready to throw the rule book at you. In this book there are no Stitch Police looking over your shoulder telling you what the rules are, and how the back of your work must be as beautiful as the front. You can nearly always start your embroidery with a knot, simply because you will nearly always have one or more layers underneath the patchwork, and padding below that, to hide a few bumps. For the same reason you can sneak around on the back of your work without finishing off after every isolated stitch (but do watch your tension so that you don't include a few puckers).

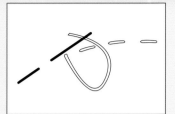

Running stitch

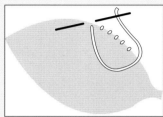

Backstitch

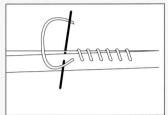

Split backstitch

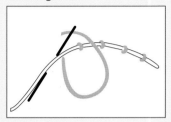

Couching

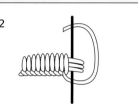

Appliqué stitch

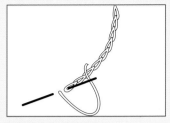

Whipstitch

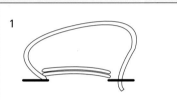

1

2

Buttonhole loop

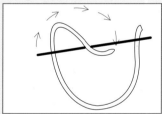

1

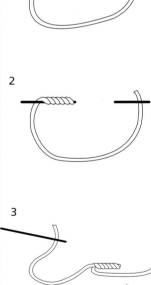

2

3

French knot

1

2

3

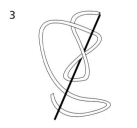

4

5

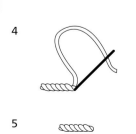

Colonial knot

Bullion stitch

Getting started

THE FIRST STEP in crazy patchwork is to sew fabrics in a crazy fashion to a foundation piece of fabric. The best choice for this foundation fabric is a lightweight calico or homespun, or light cotton, such as a cheap lawn. Whatever you choose, make sure it has enough body to support the patchwork, but is light and flexible enough to make embroidering the surface easy, rather than a chore. Wash the foundation fabric to remove any sizing.

The foundation fabric should always be at least 5 cm larger on every side than the area of the finished patchwork. This makes the surface easier to work with, and gives you room to manoeuvre if something goes wrong. The outline of the piece to be made is first drawn onto the foundation fabric in pencil.

For most pieces, the foundation fabric is then covered with Pellon, a dense, lightweight padding, like quilt batting, which is tacked into position — tack around the edges on the pencil line and across the centre from corner to corner. When applying the crazy patchwork pieces, always extend beyond the outline, as this will save you having to add a piece later in an empty corner, or allow you to choose the best selection of colours and shapes to work with.

If you do not want a padded surface, because you intend to pad beneath the fabric, or because, for example, the extra layer will be difficult to turn to the back of a box lid, simply omit the Pellon and work directly onto the foundation fabric. To create a more stable surface for the embroidery, you can iron a piece of lightweight fusible interfacing onto the back of your finished patchwork base before starting the embroidery. Alternatively, you can leave the back plain, as I did for the Christmas table runner (since this was to be quilted), and for the box lid and brooches in this book. The crazy patchwork for the ocean bag (page 39) could be backed with interfacing, as well as, or instead of being padded with Pellon, as this would give the bag a little firmness. The preferred method is given in the instructions for each project, but you may feel more comfortable with one particular method and you should use whichever is easiest for you, regardless of the instructions.

The crazy patchwork base for every project in this book is made in the same way: follow the diagrams and accompanying text on pages 8–9. Refer also to the photographs of the finished pieces as a guide to their construction.

The patchwork construction method specifies a 5 mm seam allowance. However, if you have a ¼ inch foot for your machine, you can use that to stitch the pieces together and trim all seams to ¼ inch (6 mm). This will not affect the size of the piece you are making. But you must *not* use a ¼ inch seam anywhere else in these projects or they will be the wrong size, and in some cases may not be able to be completed successfully.

Getting out of a tight corner

No matter how carefully you work, it sometimes happens that you find yourself locked in a corner with no escape, or you might even have created a bald patch where the foundation fabrics shows through, or have ended up with a very l-o-o-o-ng edge of fabric to cover. Never fear, there are solutions at hand!

CRAZY WISDOM

Patchwork books nearly always tell you to wash fabrics before you use them, in case they shrink or bleed dye later when you wash your work. Apart from the foundation fabric, I never wash fabrics, not even patchwork cottons, for crazy. Many of the silks and synthetics you are likely to use are not washable: they must be dry-cleaned. And most crazy projects are not likely to be going in and out of the washing machine anyway. Any pieces you make from this book should be spot-cleaned if they become marked, but generally you should keep them dust-free by regularly shaking them, or vacuuming with the nozzle of the vacuum hose covered with one or two layers of nylon cut from discarded pantyhose. Hang pieces in the shade to air them, and wash cushion inserts. If cleaning is necessary, remove three-dimensional charms and fancy buttons.

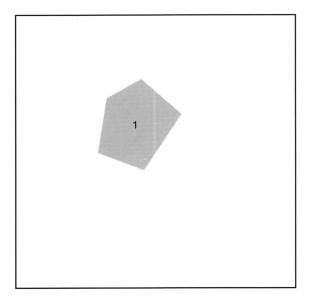

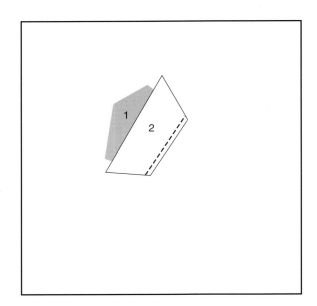

1 Cut an irregularly shaped, five-sided piece of fabric to start. Cut a fairly large piece for a large project and a smaller piece for a smaller project. Place it slightly off-centre. Don't use a dominant pattern or colour, or the eye will go straight to it, like the centre of a bull's eye.

2 Place a second piece of fabric along one side of the first piece, right sides together, aligning the raw edges of the side to be sewn. Machine stitch 5 mm (or ¼ inch if you are using a ¼ inch foot) from the raw edges. Trim the seam allowance to 5 mm if necessary.

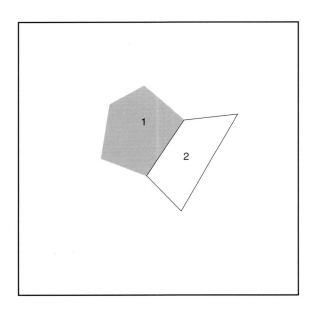

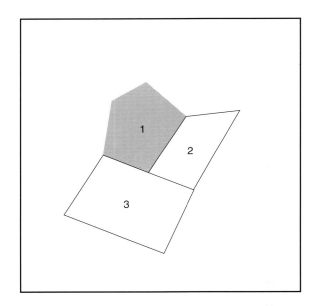

3 Fold out piece number 2 to the right side, and press lightly. You can use an iron on a low heat setting, even when you have a padding of Pellon, but use only the tip of the iron and don't set it down on the Pellon. If you are using synthetic fabrics, be very careful with the iron: test the fabric first, keep the iron on the lowest setting, and use an ironing cloth.

4 Stitch a third piece of fabric along the raw edge of pieces 1–2, aligning the raw edges. The edge of piece 2 is not perfectly aligned with the raw edge of piece 1 (see diagram 3), so you should either align it with the edge of piece 1 or choose a new line for both. Trim the seam allowance to 5 mm, cutting away any excess from the pieces. Fold out, and press lightly on the right side.

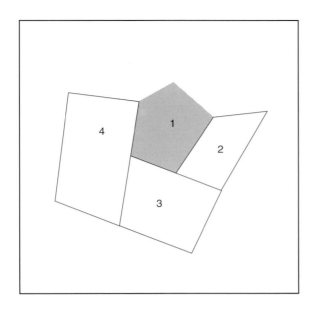

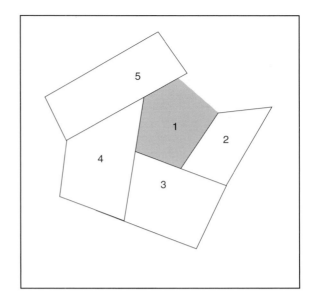

5   Proceed clockwise around piece 1. Stitch the fourth piece along the edge of 3–1, aligning the raw edges as far as possible, and trimming the seam allowance to 5 mm, cutting away any excess from piece 3. Fold out, and press lightly on the right side.

6   Add piece 5 along the edge of pieces 4–1, and trim and press in the same manner as before. Each time, add a larger piece of fabric than you expect to need, and don't trim it to shape before adding it.

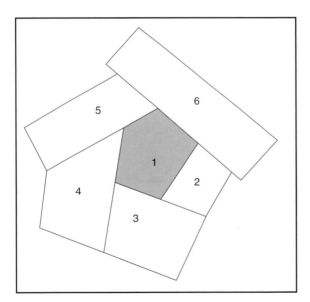

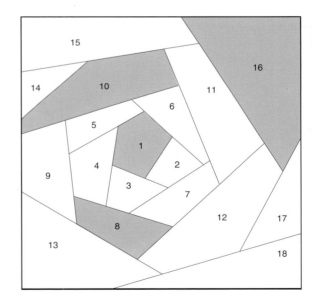

7   Add piece 6 along the edge of pieces 5–1–2, and trim and press in the same manner as before. Then add piece 7 along the edge of pieces 6–2–3. Continue adding pieces of fabric, working in a clockwise direction, until the whole area marked on the foundation fabric is covered, and patches extend a little beyond the marked line.

8   The completed crazy patchwork block, showing the order in which pieces were added. Notice how adding each round of fabrics can be used to alter the shape of pieces in the previous round. In addition, the pieces can be trimmed to a new shape after they have been sewn in place to give new edges for the next round to be attached to — this was done to pieces 10 and 12 — and to help avoid a concentric look.

To take the last problem first: it is very easy to end up with increasingly long edges as you approach the outside of a large piece. You can avoid the problem by recutting the edges of your strips after they have been added, to create new edges for the next row — this is why it is always a good idea to use larger pieces of fabric than you think you will need. But you can also solve the long-edge problem after it has happened. Rather than add another, even longer, piece of fabric in the next round, you can join several small pieces of fabric together in a strip, making each seam slightly angled. Add this piece just as you would an ordinary strip of fabric. Sometimes a fabric with a large check or stripe will create the look of more than one fabric, especially if you use embroidery to emphasise the lines between the colours. And if you decide just to add that long strip, make sure you recut the outer edge so you won't end up with an even longer strip in the next row. Make sure it's a plain or fairly plain fabric that will allow you to capitalise on the large space by filling it with embroidery (ribbon embroidery, especially, works well here). Or you could couch ribbon or braid onto the strip to divide it into two or more pieces, or couch a meandering trail of silk ribbon, chenille or bouclé thread, or a piece of lace, over the area.

If you detect a bald patch, the best solution is appliqué. Cut a motif from fabric, allowing a little extra fabric all round, and apply paper-backed fusible web to the back (refer to *Victorian tiles* on page 32 for details of this method). Cut out along the edges of the motif and press it into place — the fusible web adheres to Pellon as well as fabric. Attach the appliqué with a decorative stitch. A fabric shape, like the shapes used in *Victorian tiles,* can be applied in the same way. Shapes can also be appliquéd in the traditional

CRAZY WISDOM

As you progress around the first patch, it is important to vary the choice of fabrics. Alternate patterns and plains at the very least. You may find, especially if you like to do lots of embroidery, that this will give you too many patterns, so vary the look by using textures, velvets and velveteens alongside almost-plain fabrics such as mottled or tone-on-tone prints, as well as checks and stripes in various sizes. Also vary colours and shades

CRAZY WISDOM

It's all very well adding large pieces of fabric to the crazy patchwork base, but it does use up a lot of fabric and create numerous small scraps. Save all these little scraps in colour-coded bags. Make them your first source when you do a crazy patchwork project, since the smallest pieces are used first, at the centre of the patchwork. And the scrap bag will be a goldmine when you need to make tiny treasures such as the brooches on pages 49–53.

manner (the appliqué stitch is shown on page 6). Or you can cut a larger piece of fabric, about the size of the other pieces being used, with a curved edge. Baste a narrow turning along the curved edge, set it in place to cover the ugly spot, and appliqué in place. Lace motifs and ribbons will also disguise baldness.

If you get stuck in a corner — where there is an inside angle, for instance — you can usually cover it with a long strip of fabric, or a strip of pieced patches, as suggested above. Or you can use a series of triangles, first stitched along one edge, and then each succeeding triangle added to the last, to create a fan shape. This will often leave a raw edge that has to be turned under and appliquéd in place, and there may be a tuft of raw edges at the point of the fan. You can cover these with appliqué (the same treatment as the bald spot) or with a lace motif or ribbon, or a large button, or a combination of these (trim away the fluff first and make sure that no bare bits will show through).

Occasionally, when you have finished a patchwork piece, you will feel unhappy with it. Don't throw it out and start all over again! Put it aside for a day or two and come back to it fresh; you are bound to see it in a different light.

Choosing your fabrics

Silks were the most favoured fabrics for nineteenth-century crazy patchwork. Today, we have an even greater range of fabrics available, but pure silks are still often the best, since they are usually easier to handle than synthetics. You won't, however, need to outlay heaps of cash to get in a good store of fabrics: some patchwork shops offer small cut pieces of fancy fabrics for crazy, and most good fabric shops will allow you to buy 10 cm pieces (cut across the full width of the fabric). While you're building up a good fabric stash, working in a restricted colour range (say, creams and golds) will also help keep costs down. Not every fabric piece in the patchwork needs to be different: remember that the addition of lace over the top of a piece, or using lines of embroidery or embroidered motifs, or ribbon and braids, will make every piece look different.

And don't neglect traditional patchwork cottons for crazy patchwork — especially if you have already got a cupboardful. The fabrics printed with gold fit in perfectly with silk and silky fabrics, as do the saturated colours, tone-on-tone prints, and mottled or marbled fabrics. Or you can work in cottons alone, as with the *Country Christmas* pieces made for this book. Dressmaking scraps can also be used. Whereas traditional patchwork requires the use of fabrics of the same weight, this is not the case in crazy, because the foundation fabric provides a firm surface for them all.

Old clothes from junk stalls and second-hand shops can also be a rich source of fabric at little cost. Let friends know you're collecting fabrics, and accept everything that's offered — you can choose what you want and pass the rest on. Once people know you are a collector and that you give all their old bits and pieces a new life, you may find yourself the recipient of all kinds of treasures.

Whatever colour scheme you choose, collect patterns and plains, and include checks and stripes. Collect different textures: include the richness of embroidered fabrics, patterned damasks, plush velvets and velveteens, the bright sheen of satins and the slubbed surfaces of dupion and Thai silks. Sheers can be included, too: they can be doubled over or basted to another fabric, such as a satin-weave silk.

Colour

Grouping colours will give you a far more beautiful result than if you simply toss in bits of everything. Consider these groupings:
- sea colours in all shades of blue, aqua, turquoise, teal, sea greens, greys and silver, with a dash of deep purple
- every shade of soft pink (not extending the range into candy pinks or fuchsia), silver, grey, pale green
- autumn tones of gold, yellow-greens, rust, russet, red, browns, orange, black

- mauves, lavenders and purples, silver, grey, grey-greens
- jewel tones in emerald and rich greens, fuchsia, ruby, purple, bright blue, gold; note that the addition of black increases the richness of these colours, and so does an occasional small piece of rusty orange (it sounds awful, but it works!)
- pastel tones of cream, yellow, apricot, pink, mauve, pale blue and soft green with grey and silver
- every variety of cream, extending into vanilla and butterscotch colours, and gold
- apricot and peach, creams, lavender, soft green, grey and silver or gold
- every shade of blue with grey and silver
- Christmas red and green, with gold
- country Christmas colours in deep rather than bright reds and green, mid and navy blue, creams and tans.

The basic tool kit

Within each project described in this book is a list of the materials needed for that project, from fabric requirements to suggested needles. Special tool requirements are also listed: sometimes you will need pinking shears, and sometimes a rotary cutter, mat and quilter's ruler will make the job easier, so all of these are listed. However, it has been assumed that you already have basic sewing equipment, such as pins and a tape measure, so these are not listed.

In all of the projects a sewing machine is used for piecing and making up. Whether you have an heirloom or a brand-new computerised machine, treat it tenderly — by cleaning and oiling before each sewing session — and it will reward you with good behaviour. Oiling before you start work ensures that the oil is spread through the machine while it is working and warm. Stitch on scrap fabric before starting work if you fear leakages. It is especially important to clean the machine before oiling, and before you start work on a very pale project — dark spots of fluff caught in the stitching can't be classed as embellishment. Also give your machine a new needle frequently (not just when you break one), as this will help ensure clean, even stitching.

A zipper foot is extremely useful for making and attaching piping (required for one project in this book), and for inserting zips (one of the projects), and this is likely to have been supplied with your machine. A walking foot, or dual-feed foot, may not have been supplied, but you may want to invest in one — it is used for nearly every project in this book. This fitting is particularly useful when dealing with the layers of fabric in crazy patchwork. It has other uses too, including attaching borders to projects, or in any sewing where the top and bottom layers may slip, and for machine quilting.

It is essential to have good dressmaking scissors that are kept for fabrics only (you will have to find the perfect place to hide them from the family). Keep a retired pair of fabric scissors or a special pair for cutting paper, template plastic and quilt batting. Smaller scissors are also a good idea for crazy patchwork, as they are handier for trimming seam allowances and cutting small pieces of fabric. Snips are essential for cutting thread — they're quicker and easier than scissors to pick up and use, and snipping the thread won't create blunt spots on your scissors.

In addition to a tape measure for general measuring, a quilter's metric ruler is very useful for making templates, cutting regular pieces of fabric and interfacing, adding seam allowances, and so on.

Window templates

A particularly useful tool in crazy patchwork is the window template. The shape of the final patchwork piece — whether a heart, a rectangle or some other shape — is cut away from the centre of a piece of template plastic. It can be used for marking the shape of the pieces, like an ordinary template, but its greatest use is in showing you exactly what the patchwork will look like when it is cut to shape — the template is simply held over the patchwork.

You can make a window template using a quilter's ruler and a waterproof marker.

Draw the outline of the finished shape of the piece to be made: for example, a rectangle for a bag or a heart for the Christmas decorations. Draw an outer rectangle or square about 3 cm outside the first line — whatever the shape of the window in the template, always make the outside edge a square or rectangle at least 3 cm larger than the window. Cut along the sides of the outer rectangle or square, then cut away the centre of the inner piece: this will make a window template

for the finished area of the patchwork. Use a hobby knife or an old rotary cutter on a cutting mat to remove the centre, or paper scissors if your plastic is thin.

The template can also be used to determine the final placement of the pattern, as well as for marking, so that you can see exactly what will be visible on the final piece

Even when the pattern is a simple square or rectangle, you will find the window template enormously helpful. Label and store your templates if you are likely to make the project again, or recycle the pieces by recutting them — and if you take a little care cutting out the centre, this plastic can also be used for smaller templates.

Straight stitch flowers

Straight stitch

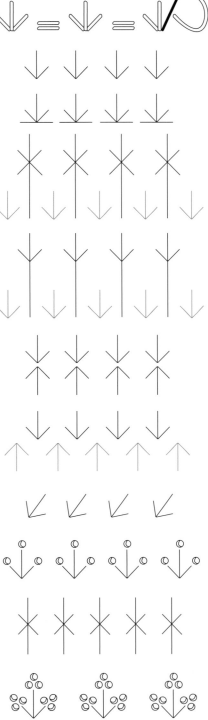

Straight stitch

Stem stitch

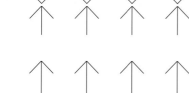

Peaches and cream

A DELICATE DOUBLE PURSE in peach and cream fabrics, this precious piece is based on a Victorian flat purse — it makes a perfect sewing project holder. The purse folds in two and is tied with a wide matching ribbon; each pocket is closed with a clear snap fastener. In the same colour scheme, a fabric-covered box has a crazy patchwork lid.

Victorian bag

Finished size

46 × 21 cm open, 16.5 × 21 cm closed

Materials

Two 30 × 25 cm pieces of foundation fabric

Two 30 × 25 cm pieces of Pellon

25 cm of 115 cm wide patterned fabric for the outer bag

25 cm of 115 cm wide lining fabric for outer bag and pockets; choose a plain silk in a colour to tone with the outer fabric

25 × 50 cm piece of fusible interfacing (optional)

25 × 50 cm piece of Pellon for padding the exterior of the bag (optional)

1.2 m of 2–3 cm wide double-sided polyester ribbon for ties

Small pieces of silks (or silky fabrics) and cottons for patchwork — in white, creams, apricot and peach; in patterns, plains and textures

Embroidery threads: silk and cotton stranded and perle threads in apricot, peach, cream, green and lavender

Scraps of lace and lace motifs

Small pieces of ribbons and light braids

Silk ribbon for embroidery

Small beads in peach, apricot, cream, clear

Beading thread

Charms (optional)

2 clear plastic snap fasteners

Ecru machine sewing thread

Crewel, milliner's, sharps and chenille needles in a variety of sizes

F pencil or Pacer pencil

Waterproof fine-tip felt pen

Chalk pencil

Sheet of template plastic

Quilter's metric ruler

Rotary cutter

Cutting mat

Sheet of A4 photocopy paper

Method

Use the template plastic and the waterproof pen to make a window template the size of the pocket (see page 12): the inner rectangle should measure 15 × 21 cm.

Use the template to draw, in pencil, a rectangle 15 × 21 cm on each piece of the foundation fabric for the two pockets. Baste a piece of Pellon over each piece.

Crazy patchwork Stitch crazy patchwork pieces over each rectangle, extending beyond the pencilled outline (see *Getting started*, pages 8–9). Use plain and patterned fabrics in a variety of shapes and sizes. Include at least one scrap of the fabric for the outer bag on each pocket. Incorporate laces, ribbons and braids as you work, so that each raw edge can be sewn into the next seam.

When the patchwork for the two pockets is completed, use the window template and the chalk pencil to mark the area of the pocket on the patchwork piece.

Embellishment Embellish the rectangle with embroidery, beads, lace motifs and charms. Stitch along every seam, and work or apply motifs in the larger areas of plain fabrics.

Stitch notes

The rose bouquet is worked in ribbon embroidery. Do three french knots in the centre of each rose, then work straight stitches around the centre, starting each one halfway along the previous stitch and extending half a stitch length beyond the end of it. Buds are french knots in ribbon, with two little straight stitches on each side; and the leaves are also straight stitches. The stems are worked in two strands of stranded cotton in stem stitch.

Use zigzag chain stitch to create the honeycomb pattern.

To finish

A seam allowance of 1 cm is used throughout. Always sew with right sides together, unless otherwise specified.

To secure When the embroidery is completed, redraw the chalk outline if necessary. Using the walking foot on the sewing machine and a longer-than-usual stitch, stitch on this line to secure the patches and any embroidery threads that will be cut in the next step. Cut out the piece 1 cm past the stitching line.

The pockets Cut two 17 × 23 cm pocket-lining pieces from the lining fabric. Stitch a pocket-lining piece and a patchwork pocket together along the marked line, leaving a 6 cm opening on one short side for turning the pocket out, but make sure you stitch all the corners.

Remove the basting threads. Lightly press the seam lines on the patchwork side: this helps lock the machine stitches and makes the seams sit better when the piece is turned out.

Turn back the edges of the opening, and lightly press on each side. It is important that you apply just the point of the iron to the seams only — don't sweep the iron all over your work, or you will flatten your embroidery.

Trim the corners, and cut away as much of the foundation fabric and Pellon as you can, including under the turn-in at the opening. Turn the pockets out, finger-pressing the seams, and ensuring that the corners are as square as you can make them without distorting them. Whipstitch the opening closed.

Assembly Make two paper patterns of the bag flap. Cut a 46 × 23 cm strip of both the lining and the outer-bag fabric.

If you wish, press iron-on interfacing to the wrong side of the outer bag. This helps keep the outer surface of the bag reasonably firm. If you use a heavyweight fabric for the outer bag you will not need to interface it; if you use a lightweight or floppy fabric, interfacing will be essential. Also cut a 46 × 23 cm strip of Pellon if you

Bag flap pattern
Actual size

wish to pad the purse, and place it behind the lining in the following instructions.

Pin the lining and outer-bag pieces right sides together, and pin the flap pattern at each end, setting the top of the curve 1 cm from the short edge of the fabric. Stitch the pieces together, stitching around the edge of the paper pattern at each end, and leaving a 10 cm opening along the long edge, keeping away from either the bag centre or the top and bottom edges.

Press, and press the opening seams open. Turn right side out through the opening, and press. Stitch the opening closed with whip-stitch, and press.

To complete the bag Place the two pockets against the outer-bag lining, about 0.5–1 cm apart. Stitch them to the outer bag by hand, using a close cretan stitch (see page 18). Stitch the snap fasteners to the tip of the bag flaps and to the corresponding position on the pockets.

Fold the ribbon in half, and stitch it to the fold on the outer bag, at the centre. Use a decorative stitch if you wish, or just a tiny running stitch or backstitch.

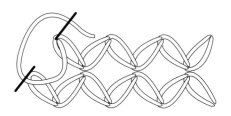

Zigzag chain stitch

Fabric-covered box

Finished size

Lid: 16 × 26 cm

Detached chain stitch flower

Materials

Rectangular box kit and extra supplies, excluding fabric, specified in its instructions (see the list of suppliers, page 71)
25 × 35 cm piece of foundation fabric
40 cm of 110 cm wide plain silk for outer box
40 cm of 110 cm wide plain or patterned silk for box lining
40 cm of 90 cm wide Pellon for padding lid and box lining
Small pieces of silks or silky and cotton fabrics for the patchwork — in peaches, apricots, creams, soft green and lavender; in plains, mottled and tone-on-tone prints, and textures
Embroidery threads: cottons, silks, metallics, synthetics, over-dyed, chenille

Silk ribbon
Small beads and sequins
Beading thread
Braids, ribbons and laces in creams
Skein of apricot no. 5 perle cotton for tassel and twisted cord
Apricot or ecru machine sewing thread
Crewel, milliner's, sharps and chenille needles in a variety of sizes
F pencil or Pacer pencil
Waterproof fine-tip felt pen
Chalk pencil
Sheet of template plastic
Quilter's metric ruler
Rotary cutter
Cutting mat

Silk ribbon roses

Cretan stitch

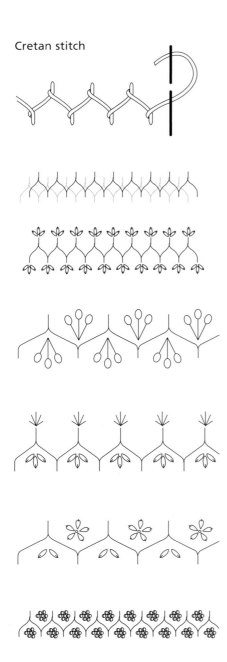

Method

First make a window template for the patchwork, which will also be a pattern for the box-lid frame (see page 12). Using the felt-tip pen, draw a rectangle measuring 13 × 23 cm onto template plastic. Use the metric quilter's ruler to draw another rectangle 1.5 cm inside that line (rectangle measures 10 × 20 cm), and another one 3 cm outside the first line (rectangle measures 19 × 29 cm). Cut out the plastic on the *outer* line.

The fabric mount Prepare the silk frame for the lid first. Cut a piece of the outer box silk measuring 19 × 29 cm, using the outer edge of the window template as the pattern. Now cut out the centre of the *template* on the line of the *innermost* rectangle. Use the template to mark this line with chalk pencil on the wrong side of the frame fabric. Now recut the *template* on the next line (the first one that was drawn). Use the template and the chalk pencil to mark this line on the wrong side of the frame fabric.

Cut out the centre of the piece of silk, cutting on the innermost chalk line. Clip the corners from the cut edge back to the chalk line 1.5 cm away. Carefully fold the edges of the innermost rectangle 1.5 cm to the wrong side, folding along the last chalk line drawn, and ensuring that the corners are sharp and no frayed threads are visible (the inner edge of the frame should measure 13 × 23 cm). Press. Baste the seam allowance in position, and set the fabric mount aside until the patchwork is finished.

Crazy patchwork Once you have made the final cut on the template (to the centre 13 × 23 cm rectangle) you have a window template for the final size of the patchwork piece.

Use the window template to outline, using pencil, the lid shape on the foundation fabric. Stitch crazy patchwork pieces over the shape, extending beyond the pencilled outline (see *Getting started*, pages 8–9). Use plain and patterned fabrics in a variety of shapes and sizes. Incorporate lace and braids as you work, so that their raw edges are sewn into the next seam.

When the patchwork is completed, use the chalk pencil and the window template to draw the outline of the final shape onto the patchwork.

Embellishment Embellish the patchwork piece with embroidery, beads and sequins, lace, ribbon and braids. Stitch every seam, and work or apply motifs in the larger areas of plain fabrics.

To secure When the embroidery is completed, redraw the chalk outline if necessary. Using the walking foot on the sewing machine and a longer-than-usual stitch, stitch along this line to secure the patches and any embroidery threads that will be cut in the next step. Cut out the piece 1.5 cm past the stitching line.

To attach the mount Place the fabric mount over the patchwork piece, and baste it to the patchwork. Attach the mount to the patchwork with a decorative stitch, such as herringbone or double herringbone or laced herringbone. Ensure that the stitches are close together to achieve a secure attachment. You may prefer to appliqué the mount in place before finishing with a decorative stitch, or machining it into position.

In *Peaches and cream* a Victorian-style double purse has
the most delicate embroidery in thread and ribbon. Similar
colours and motifs decorate the lid of a box made from a
kit. The box is covered and lined with silk (page 15).

To finish

Make up the box and lining following the instructions in the box
kit. Ensure that the patchwork lid and mount are carefully centred
over the covered box lid.

Peaches and cream

A country Christmas

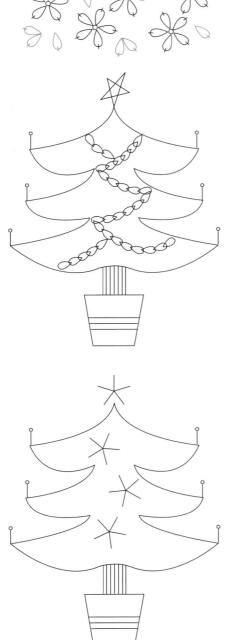

THE SOFT COLOURS of country-style patchwork fabrics give a look that is different from the bright reds and greens we usually see at Christmas. Using the same family of fabrics, for the table runner three large crazy patchwork blocks are joined with quilted sashing and borders. In keeping with the country style, and also to keep the runner surface flat and functional, beads and charms are not used.

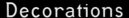

Decorations

Finished sizes

Bell: 9.5 cm high
Diamond: 11.5 cm high
Square: each side, 7.5 cm

Heart: 9.5 cm high
Stocking: 11 cm high
Star: 13 cm at widest point

Materials

20 cm square piece of foundation fabric for each decoration

20 cm square piece of Pellon for each decoration

15 cm square piece of cotton fabric for backing each decoration

20 cm piece of narrow ribbon or an embroidery thread for hanging each decoration

Small pieces of cotton fabrics — in patterns, checks, stripes and plains; Christmas colours — for patchwork

Embroidery threads: silk and cotton stranded and perle

threads, golds, rich blue, red and green, and variegated stranded threads, or colours to suit your fabric choice

Small pieces of ribbon and light braids (optional)

Small beads and charms (optional)

Beading thread (optional)

Ecru or grey machine sewing thread

Fibrefill

Crewel, milliner's and sharps needles in a variety of sizes

F pencil or Pacer pencil

Waterproof fine-tip felt pen

Chalk pencil

Sheet of template plastic

Method

Note that templates are finished sizes; you must add seam allowances when cutting out the final shape.

Trace the pattern pieces (page 21) onto template plastic using the waterproof pen, and cut them out, or make a window template for each shape (see page 12). Draw a 7.5 cm square and make a template for the square decoration.

Christmas decoration templates, actual size. Add 5 mm seam allowances when cutting out pieces to make up.

Use a pencil to trace around each template onto a square of foundation fabric.

Baste a piece of Pellon over each piece of base fabric.

Crazy patchwork Stitch crazy patchwork pieces over each shape, extending beyond the pencilled outline (see *Getting started*, pages 8–9). Use plain and patterned fabrics in a variety of shapes and sizes.

If you are including picture prints, you will probably find it easiest to make one of these the first patch. Don't try to add fabric on every side of the first patch though, as the decorations are small. Make your picture piece extend over the seam line on at least one side. Use lots of plains to give space for embroidery.

Keep seam lines away from the notch of the heart or the points of the star, or wherever there is a sharp curve or point, and away from the opening for turning through. If you wish, incorporate ribbon and braids as you work, so that their raw edges can be sewn into the next seam.

Embellishment When the patchwork is completed, use the template to draw the outline of the appropriate shape on the right side of the patchwork base — choose the placement that will show off the fabrics and keep seam lines away from vital points. Make sure you have at least a 5 mm clearance from the edge of the work, for seam allowances.

Embellish each decoration with embroidery, extending a little past the seam line. Stitch every seam, and work motifs in the larger areas of plain fabrics. If you wish, add beads and charms last.

To finish

A 5 mm seam allowance is used throughout. Always sew with right sides together, unless otherwise specified.

To secure When the embroidery is completed, redraw the chalk outline if necessary. Using the walking foot on the sewing machine and a longer-than-usual stitch, stitch on this line to secure the patches and any embroidery threads that will be cut in the next step. Cut out the piece 5 mm past the stitching line.

The shapes Stitch each patchwork piece to the backing fabric — leave the backing piece as a square for easier sewing — machine sewing along the stitching line, and using the standard stitch size on your machine, or one a little smaller. This ensures a smooth outline and keeps stitches invisible when the decoration is turned through and filled (this is no time to use a larger stitch just because it's easier to undo!).

Leave an opening along one side in the following places for turning:

- on the heart and the bell, about the centre of one of the long sides;
- for the star, along the side of one point, away from the inner curve and the point — this leaves a small but adequate opening;
- for the stocking, along the top, but ensure that the corners are stitched;
- for the square and diamond, along any straight side, but make sure all corners are stitched.

Double stitch at the start and end of the seam on each side of the opening to prevent unravelling when you pull through and fill.

CRAZY WISDOM

When you have turned out any shape, use the tip of your finger inside the shape to help smooth out the edges, particularly the curves. Use a blunt instrument to push corners very gently into sharp points. (I have to confess that I use curve-tipped scissors to do this, but it's perilously easy to pierce your fabric, so be very careful!)

Once you have turned the piece through, finger-press by holding the seam between the thumb and forefinger of each hand and gently rolling the seam backwards and forwards, flattening and opening the seam fully to ensure that the backing rolls towards the back. This will give you a much better edge than pressing with an iron ever will.

Country reds and greens are used in this runner and group of decorations for *A country Christmas* projects (page 20). ▶

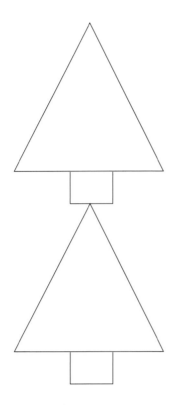

Quilting motif
for sashing

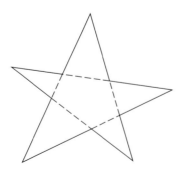

Quilting motif for cornerstones

Finger-press the seams only, and gently press open the seam allowances of the opening.

To complete the shapes Cut out each piece about 5 mm from the stitching line. Snip into notches and around curves, and trim corners and points. Grade the seam allowances and trim away most of the foundation fabric and the Pellon.

Turn through (first pull the corner furthest from the opening), and stuff lightly with fibrefill.

Stitch the opening closed with whipstitch. Stitch the thread through, or attach the ribbon at, the suspension point for each decoration.

Table runner

Finished size

37 x 97 cm; each block is 25 cm square

Materials

Three 35 cm square pieces of foundation fabric

40 cm of 110 cm wide cotton fabric for sashing and borders

25 cm square piece of cotton fabric for cornerstones

50 cm of 110 cm wide patterned cotton fabric for backing

50 × 110 cm piece of batting, not too firm or thick

25 cm of 110 cm wide patterned fabric for binding

Small pieces of cotton patchwork fabrics in Christmas prints, or the selection of your choice, in a variety of patterns, picture prints, tone-on-tone prints and plains

Embroidery threads: silk and cotton stranded and perle threads, variegated stranded threads in country rose, reds, greens, blues and tans, or colours to suit your fabric choice, including variegated threads

Grey machine sewing thread for construction, or a colour to suit your fabric choice

Light-coloured thread for basting, or safety pins

Quilting thread in green, red, grey or black

Crewel needles in a variety of sizes

Betweens needle size 8–12 for quilting

F pencil or Pacer pencil

Waterproof fine-tip felt pen

Chalk pencil

Sheet of template plastic

Quilter's metric ruler

Rotary cutter

Cutting mat

Method

Use the template plastic and the waterproof pen to make a window template the size of the block (see page 12): the inner square should measure 25 cm on each side; the outer edge should be 3 cm larger on each side.

Use the template to draw a 25 cm square in pencil on each piece of the foundation fabric. No Pellon is used for the patchwork block.

Crazy patchwork Stitch crazy patchwork pieces over each square, extending beyond the pencilled outline (see *Getting started*, pages 8–9). Use plain and patterned fabrics in a variety of shapes and sizes. If you like to do lots of embroidery, include plenty of plain or tone-on-tone pieces in the patchwork.

When the patchwork is completed, use the window template

Braids, laces and ribbons are usually best incorporated in crazy patchwork when you are preparing the patchwork base, because the raw edges can be covered by the next piece of fabric that is added. However, if you need to add these pieces later, there is a solution — but you must do it before you embroider any of the seams.

Use snips or very fine-pointed embroidery scissors to cut individual stitches between patches at the points where you want to insert the ribbon, lace or braid. Undo as little as possible, and carefully remove the loose threads (tweezers will help). Gently slip the end of the ribbon in at one end, pin it along the seam, and slip it in at the other end. Use a plain or fancy stitch to attach the ribbon along the seam, and make any adjustment that is necessary at each end of the ribbon. The seams that you have opened will be secured again when you embroider over them.

and chalk pencil to outline a 25 cm square on the right side of each patchwork block.

Embellishment Embellish the block with embroidery in stranded silks and cottons, and silk and cotton perle threads. Use a variety of golds and soft Christmas and country colours. Stitch every seam, and work motifs in the larger areas of plain or tone-on-tone fabrics.

Stitch notes

The Christmas trees are worked with stem stitch outlines (two strands of stranded cotton), with a chain stitch garland on one, and five-pointed straight stitch stars on the other. The candles are made with a couple of straight stitches and a french knot on top, or a small bugle bead with a seed bead on top. Silk ribbon decorations could look attractive here too. Christmas trees are also worked in fly stitch.

Add ribbon bows to angels' hair, and decorate their clothing with embroidery stitches.

Rows of palestrina knots (see page 27) decorate some seams.

To finish

A 1 cm seam allowance is included in measurements throughout — this is larger than is usual with patchwork, because of the thickness of the crazy block. You can trim the seam allowance back to 5 mm once the blocks and sashing are joined. Don't trim the outer edges, though, as the binding is intended to enclose the full 1 cm width. The foundation fabric can be trimmed virtually to the seam line to reduce bulk. Always work with right sides together, unless otherwise specified.

To secure Use the chalk pencil and window template to redraw the 25 cm square on the top of each crazy patchwork block, if necessary. Stitch around each block on this line using the walking foot on your machine and a longer-than-usual stitch — this will anchor any embroidery threads that are cut in the next step and help keep the patches flat.

Use the rotary cutter and quilter's ruler to cut out the blocks 1 cm from the marked square (making a 27 cm square block).

Assembly Cut ten strips of sashing fabric measuring 7 × 27 cm, and eight squares from the cornerstone fabric measuring 7 × 7 cm.

Stitch a sashing strip to the left-hand side of each block. Press the seam allowance, using only the tip of the iron, towards the sashing — follow this pattern throughout to ensure that all seam allowances are pressed away from the patchwork block.

Stitch a cornerstone to the left-hand side of a sashing strip — make six of these strips. Stitch a cornerstone-sashing piece to the top and bottom of each block. Stitch the remaining two cornerstones to each end of the last sashing strip, and stitch it to the right-hand side of the right-hand block.

Join the three block–sashing pieces together. Gently press the seams only, using the tip of the iron.

Quilting patterns Trace the quilting patterns — the Christmas tree for the sashing and the star for the cornerstones — onto template plastic: you need to trace only one tree, and mark the dashed lines on the star on the template — these won't be traced onto the fabric as they are short enough to be filled 'by eye'. Cut out the shapes, and use a chalk pencil to trace around them onto the sashing and cornerstones.

Basting Cut a piece of backing fabric measuring 50 × 110 cm, and press it to ensure that it is wrinkle free. Lay it out, wrong side up, on a work table, and use masking tape to hold it in position, making sure that the fabric is straight and taut, but not stretched or distorted.

Lay the piece of batting on top. Lay the completed patchwork top on top of this, right side up, and centred over the two bottom pieces. Secure the top to the table, but don't pull it too tight. Baste or pin the three layers together, starting at the centre.

Quilting Quilting from the centre outwards, too, quilt in the ditch around each of the three blocks and the cornerstones. Use a gold perle thread to work little stars or other suitable motifs at points over the block, working through all three layers to tie the runner. Just inside the intersections of seams is a good spot to tie. Quilt the sashing and cornerstones. Remove the pins as you work towards the edge, but leave the outer row in place until the binding is pinned. Remove all the basting threads after the binding is attached.

Binding Cut three 6 cm strips on the straight grain across the full width of the fabric. Join them together to make a strip 3 m long. Fold the strip in half along its length, right side out, to make a double binding 3 cm wide. Pin the binding around the edges of the quilt, matching the raw edges, and stitch all the layers together 1 cm from the edge, mitring the corners (see page 69).

When you have stitched the binding in place, join the two ends of the binding together. Turn the folded edge of the binding to the back, aligning the fold with the line of stitching, and hem in place.

(see page 69)

Palestrina knot

1

2

3

Sheaf stitch

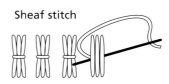

CRAZY WISDOM

To keep up the simple country look, these pieces were decorated with embroidery only — in stranded cotton or silk — with very few beads and charms. Stitches only were used to embellish the runner, in order to keep the surface smooth and give a stable base for anything that might be set on it.

If country style is not to your taste, start with different fabric choices: try silks in gold and white, or jewel colours, or silver, blue and white, or traditional Christmas colours. By adding all sorts of treasures, buttons, beads, ribbon and charms, not to mention metallic threads, you could easily create a sumptuous, glittering look. Or try rich Victorian colours, and embellish with ribbons and lace. If you make the matching runner, you should still keep three-dimensional effects to a minimum.

Only one side of the decorations has crazy patchwork, as the pieces would be impossible to turn through with crazy on both sides.

A country Christmas

Victorian tiles

INSPIRED BY A VICTORIAN original, this unusual crazy patchwork piece is made up of scattered appliqué pieces, attached to the background fabric and embellished with decorative stitches, with the spaces in between filled with the lavish embroidery so typical of crazy patchwork. This version takes a modern approach to appliqué, using paper-backed fusible web. It is a throw, or coverlet, which is backed, but not padded or quilted.

Finished size

91 × 112 cm

Materials

1 m of 110 cm wide medium-weight cream silk (it needs to have a certain amount of weight to support the appliqué and embroidery; also avoid satin weave fabrics)

1.2 m of 110 cm wide medium-weight silk for the backing

1.2 m of 110 cm wide medium-weight striped silk

2–3 m of paper-backed fusible web (the amount needed will depend on the width of the web available and on the amount and number of fabrics used for appliqué shapes)

10 cm square pieces of silk and silky fabrics, plains, textures and prints; in lights, mediums and darks (smaller and odd-shaped pieces can also be used, but each piece will need to have a matching piece of fusible web cut for it)

Stranded silk thread (Madeira, Au ver à soie, or Waterlilies by Caron) in a variety of gold colours

Ecru machine sewing thread for construction

Light-coloured thread or safety pins for basting.

No. 9 or 10 crewel needles

Roll of baking paper, such as Gladbake

Anti-fray product, such as Fray Stoppa (optional)

F or Pacer pencil

Waterproof fine-tip felt pen

Chalk pencil

2–3 sheets of template plastic

Quilter's metric ruler

Rotary cutter

Cutting mat

Method

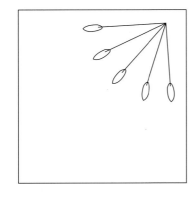

Using the rotary cutter, cut three strips of the cream silk measuring 93 × 20 cm (add a little extra if you wish, to allow for the silk fraying, then recut to the correct size before making up; you could also treat the edges with a tiny amount of anti-fray product).

Templates Using the waterproof marker, trace the appliqué shapes onto template plastic and cut them out (you do not need window templates for this project). Add some squares, rectangles, triangles and circles (template shapes not included in this book). Enlarge or reduce the shapes on a photocopier if you want a greater variety of sizes or to vary the size of the project.

Preparation for appliqué Cut squares of paper-backed fusible web a little under 10 cm square.

Place a large sheet of baking paper on the ironing board. Lay out the 10 cm squares of fabric, right side down, on the paper. Place

Templates for *Victorian tiles*, actual size

Templates for *Victorian tiles*, actual size

An old style is revived with a modern twist: all the appliqué shapes are first attached using paper-backed fusible web. An abundance of embroidery around, on and between the appliqué shapes makes *Victorian tiles* a most enjoyable project to work (page 28).

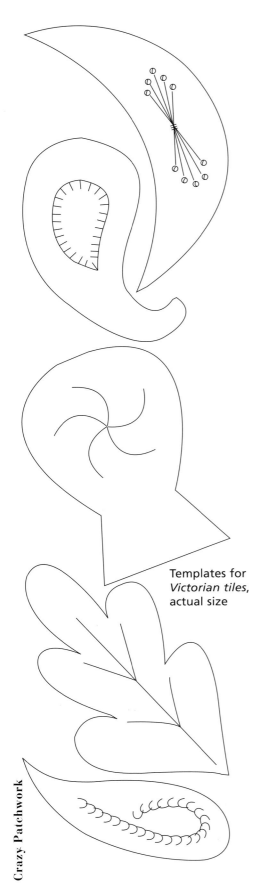

Templates for *Victorian tiles*, actual size

a square of paper-backed fusible web on top of each one, the shiny or web side down. Place a sheet of baking paper over the top of the fabric-web sandwiches. Press with a hot iron. Lift and set down the iron, holding it briefly in place to ensure that the web attaches to the fabric.

When all the pieces have been pressed, lift off the top piece of baking paper and check that fusion has taken place — the edges of fabric and the fabrics at the edge of the board are most likely to need re-pressing. Crêpes and heavy-weight or textured fabrics are also reluctant to accept the web, and so will often need re-pressing too.

Making the shapes Using the pencil, trace around the templates onto the paper back of each fabric-web sandwich. Ensure that you use a range of shapes — angles and curves — of different sizes on a variety of fabrics. When you have a good collection, cut out the shapes with small, sharp scissors. Working on the ironing board, lay out the shapes on one of the strips of silk, balancing shapes, sizes, patterns and plains, darks and lights, and keeping at least 1 cm from each edge of the fabric.

When you are satisfied with the arrangement, lift each shape, gently remove the paper from the back, and set the piece back in its place. Cover the whole piece with a sheet of baking paper, and press the pieces into place, as described above.

Allow to cool a little, and check that each piece has adhered — it's very easy to forget to remove the backing paper, and these pieces will flutter away if you lift the silk without checking that they have fused first. Spot press any that need a little extra heat. Also spot press any pieces that start to lift when you are sewing — remember to protect your iron by covering the area with baking paper.

CRAZY WISDOM

Paper-backed fusible web is a wonderful product (available under a number of trade names, including Vliesofix and HeatnBond). It allows you to iron a glue to the wrong side of a piece of fabric that is to be appliquéd to another fabric. Iron the *shiny* side of the web to the *wrong* side of the appliqué fabric. Draw the pattern or shape in pencil on the paper side. When you are ready to use the piece, cut out the shape on the pencil line and gently peel off the paper back. Put the shape, right side up, on the right side of the background fabric and press it into place. Use an edge stitch — buttonhole stitch is ideal — to appliqué it in place. A heavier weight product that does not require the additional security of stitching is also available, but it is not suitable for tiles.

When using paper-backed fusible web always press fabrics between two sheets of baking paper, as the web sometimes oozes out and can make a mess of your iron and ironing board. Discard the paper after pressing each batch: if a little web gets onto the paper it can easily find its way onto the right side of your fabrics, which are a lot more precious than a little baking paper. Of course, if you *do* make a mess, you can often disguise it by pressing another appliqué shape over the damaged area to make a new pattern, or hiding it with embroidery.

Stitch notes

Stitch all the pieces in place using a single strand of stranded silk thread, of any brand. A single strand of stranded cotton is too fine, and two threads too thick for silks, but one strand of silk thread is perfect. If you wish to make the project in cottons, use two strands of stranded cotton. A single strand of silk is also used for all the embroidery on and between the shapes.

Appliqué Start work on the shapes at the edges of the silk strips and work towards the centre. Add the embroidery to the pieces and the spaces only after all the shapes have been attached.

Stitches used to attach the shapes include herringbone, cross, chevron, cretan, feather, straight feather, closed feather and all the varieties of buttonhole stitch. Work them in a range of sizes and with different spacing.

Embellishment Any pattern, motif or stitch can be used on or between the shapes. Some suggestions for shapes for the patterns are included on the templates. Trails of single feather stitch are particularly useful for weaving through narrow spaces.

To finish

When all three appliqué strips are complete, trim them if necessary to 93 × 20 cm, which includes 1 cm seam allowances. Cut four strips from the striped fabric measuring 93 × 16.5 cm, which includes 1 cm seam allowances. Seam the pieces together — stripe, cream, stripe, cream, stripe, cream, stripe.

Basting Baste the backing and top of the coverlet together, or join them with safety pins.

Binding Cut five 1 m × 6 cm strips from the striped or cream fabric for the binding. Join the pieces together at a 45 degree angle. Fold the binding in half along its length, right side out, to make a double binding 3 cm wide. Pin the binding around the edges of the coverlet, matching the raw edges, and stitch all the layers together 1 cm from the edge, starting well away from a corner, and mitring the corners (see page 69). When you have stitched the binding in place, join the two ends of the binding together. Turn the folded edge of the binding to the back, aligning the fold with the line of stitching, and hem in place.

CRAZY WISDOM

Part of the fun of this project comes from working with beautiful silk fabrics, with their rich colours and sheen, and even tiny scraps of fabric can be used. However, if you have a cupboard bulging with patchwork fabrics, you could make this project in cottons. Choose a striped fabric to determine your colour scheme, or create one from strips of fabric; use a tone-on-tone cream fabric for the appliqué strips, and patchwork prints and plains for the shapes. Or why not try a black or navy blue background and rich jewel-like colours, whether in silks or cotton fabrics?

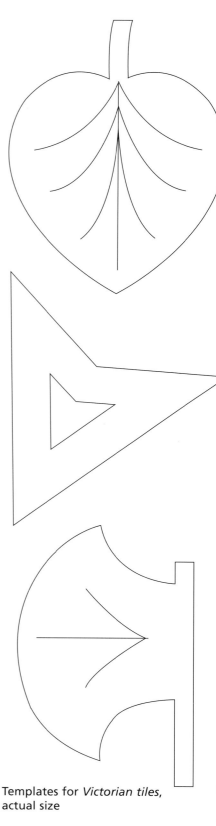

Templates for *Victorian tiles*, actual size

Buttonhole stitch

Closed buttonhole stitch

Crossed buttonhole stitch

Close buttonhole stitch

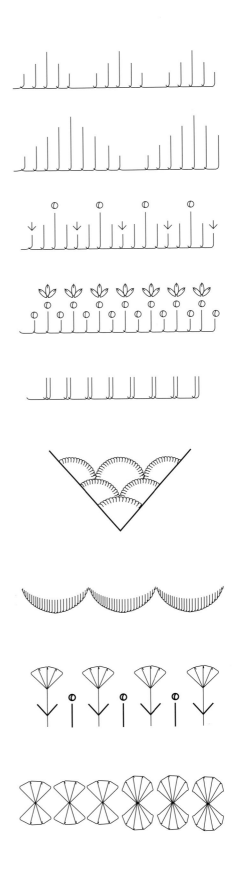

The deep blue sea

A COLLECTION OF STITCHER'S essentials is created in the blues and turquoises of the sea. Richly coloured silks are combined with patchwork cottons in intense colours or with marine patterns. Sea anemones, spouting whales, schools of tiny fish, starfish, sea fans and other oceanic motifs decorate the surfaces of a pincushion, a scissor case and a bag to store them in. The photograph on the cover of this book shows these motifs — and more — in greater detail. Charms of sea creatures are added to make this a busy underwater world. A needlecase in the same fabrics omits the marine motifs, to show that you don't have to be fishy to enjoy working with these gloriously rich colours.

Finished sizes

Scissor case: 13.5 cm long
Pincushion: 10 cm square
Bag: 20 × 16 cm
Needlecase: 7 × 16 cm (folded)

Materials

40 cm of 110 cm wide foundation fabric (all pieces)
60 cm of 90 cm wide Pellon (all pieces)
40 cm of 115 cm wide plain or patterned fabric for backing and lining (all pieces)
14 cm square of doctor flannel (needlecase)
1.3 m of rat-tail cord (bag)
1 skein of no. 5 perle cotton for twisted cord (pincushion and scissor case — optional)
Small pieces of silks or silky fabrics for patchwork — in all shades of blue, aqua, teal, turquoise and sea greens, and dark purple; in patterns, plains, mottled and tone-on-tone prints, and textures —

and patchwork cottons in intense shades of the same colours or with marine motifs
Embroidery threads: silk and cotton stranded and perle threads; variegated stranded threads, or colours to suit your fabric choice; metallics, synthetics
Silk ribbon in sea colours
Small beads in gold and sea colours, and clear
Beading thread
Charms of marine animals and motifs
Small amount of fibrefill or wool scraps or wool batting scraps (pincushion)
Small button (needlecase)

10 cm square of ultrasuede (scissor case)
Dark-blue machine sewing thread
Crewel, milliner's, sharps and chenille needles in a variety of sizes
20 cm square piece of firm cardboard (scissor case)
Clear-drying craft glue, such as 450 adhesive
F pencil or Pacer pencil
Waterproof fine-tip felt pen
Chalk pencil
Sheet of template plastic
Quilter's metric ruler
Rotary cutter
Cutting mat
Pinking shears

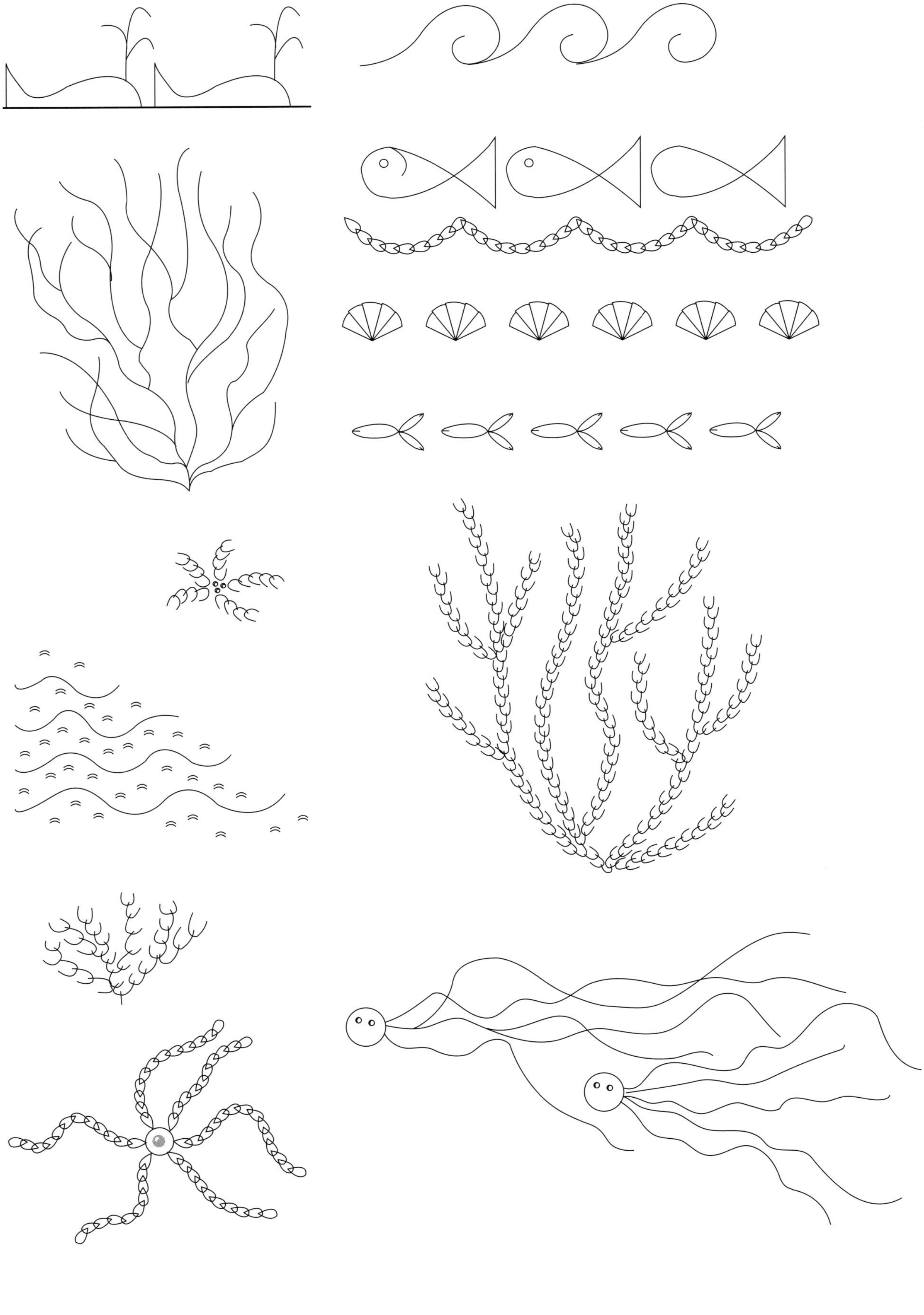

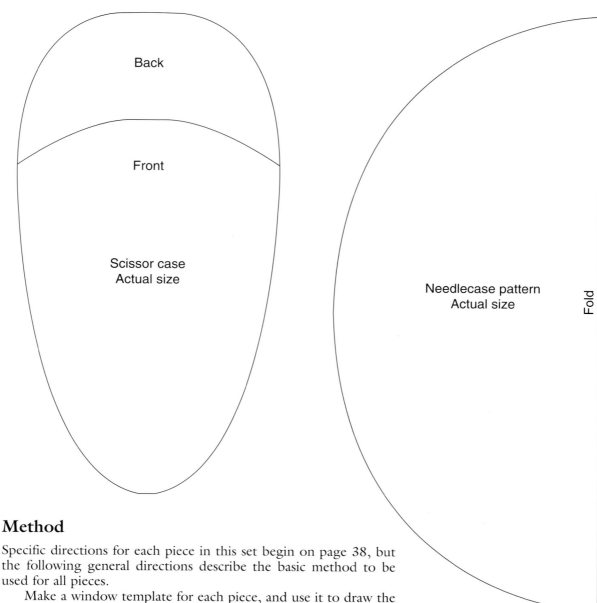

Back

Front

Scissor case
Actual size

Needlecase pattern
Actual size

Fold

Method

Specific directions for each piece in this set begin on page 38, but the following general directions describe the basic method to be used for all pieces.

Make a window template for each piece, and use it to draw the shape on foundation fabric in pencil. Baste a piece of Pellon over each piece.

Crazy patchwork Stitch crazy patchwork pieces over each piece, extending beyond the pencilled outline (see *Getting started*, pages 8–9). Use plain and patterned fabrics in a variety of shapes and sizes. Include plenty of plain and mottled fabrics to give ample space for embroidery.

Embellishment When the patchwork is completed, draw the outline of the item on the right side of the patchwork base, using the window template and a chalk pencil. Embellish the patchwork piece with embroidery, beads and charms. Stitch every seam, and work or apply motifs in the larger areas of plain fabrics.

To secure When the embroidery is completed, redraw the chalk outline if necessary. Using the walking foot on the sewing machine and a longer-than-usual stitch, stitch along this line to secure the

The perfect filler to use in pincushions is wool, because, even in processed woollen yarn, enough of the natural oil remains to keep pins smooth and rust free. If you do a lot of wool embroidery or knitting, save your scraps for stuffing pincushions. Scraps of wool batting also make a good pincushion filling, as this has the same natural qualities as wool yarn with the added advantage of a springy texture.

patches and any embroidery threads that will be cut in the next step. Cut out the piece 1 cm past the stitching line. Remove basting threads.

For making up the pieces, a 1 cm seam allowance is used throughout. Always work with right sides together, unless otherwise specified.

Stitch notes

Work schools or lines of tiny fish with three detached chain stitches.

Make octopus bodies with small shell or mother-of-pearl buttons, adding two little beads for eyes. Make their tentacles in long wavy lines with stem stitch in variegated threads. (If buttons are going to be close to seams, don't attach them until after the seam has been stitched — but before the piece is finished or the pincushion stuffed.)

Use stem stitch to make waves, whales, shark fins and fish outlines. Sea stars can be made in french knots. Brittle stars have a sequin and bead at the centre, then 'legs' of feather, chain or stem stitch.

Scallop shells are made with buttonhole stitch. Use feather stitch, fly stitch or stem stitch to create sea fans, sea ferns and fan coral — variegated threads are particularly good for these shapes, and so is silk ribbon.

Sprinkle pairs of beads to represent fish eyes among the seaweed, and clear beads to suggest air bubbles. Create a deep-sea diver in black silk ribbon. Use tiny sequins to create a fish's body. Use paper-backed fusible web to attach marine motifs cut from fabric.

Pincushion

Use the template plastic and the waterproof pen to make a window template the size of the pincushion (see page 12): the inner square should measure 10 cm square, and the outer square should be 16 cm on each side.

Cut a 15 cm square of foundation fabric and Pellon. Mark a 10 cm square on the foundation fabric, using the window template. Follow the general directions given above (pages 37–8) to complete the patchwork piece.

Making up Cut a 12 cm square of backing fabric. Stitch the backing fabric and the patchwork block together along the stitching line, leaving a 4 cm opening along one of the side edges, and ensuring that all corners are stitched.

Gently press the seams with the tip of the iron only, and press back the seam allowances at the opening. Clip the corners and grade the seam allowances, cutting the Pellon and foundation fabric almost to the seam line.

Turn the pincushion through, pulling the opposite point through first. Finger-press (see page 22). Stuff with fibrefill, wool scraps or scraps of wool batting. Close the opening with whipstitch (see page 6).

Cord edge If you want to edge the pincushion with a cord, use the perle cotton to make a twisted cord 90 cm long (see page 68), and attach it to the edge of the pincushion using whipstitch in the same colour thread as the cord. Tie a bow where the ends meet, and knot and fray the ends.

Needlecase, bag, scissor case and pincushion are worked in the richest of ocean colours. Marine motifs are embroidered and charms added to give this collection of stitcher's essentials the look of *The deep blue sea* (page 35).

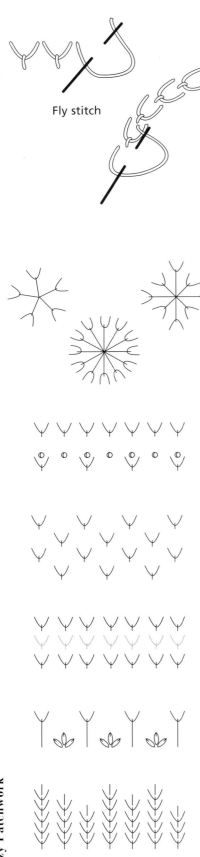

Fly stitch

Needlecase

Make a paper pattern of the whole needlecase shape and make a window template from it (see page 12). Cut a 25 × 30 cm rectangle of foundation fabric and Pellon, and draw the needlecase shape onto the foundation fabric. Follow the general directions given above (pages 37–8) to complete the patchwork piece.

Making up Using the paper pattern, and adding a 1 cm seam allowance, cut out a needlecase shape in lining fabric and Pellon. Stitch the Pellon, the backing fabric and the patchwork block together along the stitching line, leaving a 4 cm opening along the back top edge, away from the folded edge.

Gently press the seams with the tip of the iron only, and press back the seam allowances at the opening. Clip the corners and grade the seam allowances, cutting the Pellon and foundation fabric almost to the seam line. Turn the needlecase through, pulling the opposite edge through first. Finger-press (see page 22). Close the opening with whipstitch (see page 6).

Stitch the small button to the front of the needlecase, about 5 mm from the top at the centre, and work a buttonhole loop (see page 6) on the top back edge to close the case.

The insert Use pinking shears to cut a piece of doctor flannel 1 cm smaller than the needlecase pattern. Use feather stitch along the centre fold line to secure the flannel inside the case.

Bag

Cut a 30 x 25 cm piece of foundation fabric and Pellon. Use the template plastic and the waterproof pen to make a window template the size of the bag (see page 12): the inner rectangle should measure 20 x 16 cm. Use the pencil to draw this shape on the foundation fabric, and baste the Pellon on top. Follow the general directions given above (pages 37–8) to complete the patchwork piece.

Backing and lining pieces Cut three rectangles measuring 22 × 18 cm in the lining/backing fabric, and one piece of Pellon measuring 22 × 18 cm. Stitch together the patchwork piece and one lining piece, leaving a gap of about 4 cm along the bottom edge, and ensuring that all corners are stitched. Grade the seams, trimming the foundation fabric and Pellon as close to the stitching line as possible. Trim the corners.

With the tip of the iron, gently press the seams only, and turn back the seam allowances at the opening. Turn through, pulling one of the farther corners through first, and finger-press the seams. Press lightly on the wrong side. Close the opening by hand.

Make the back piece in the same manner, with two pieces of lining/backing fabric and the Pellon.

Making up Join the two bag pieces together along the side and bottom edges using whipstitch (see page 6). Stitch the rat-tail cord around these edges, using whipstitch in a matching or complementary colour. Push the two ends of the cord into the inside of the bag along the bottom edge, overlapping them slightly, or knot them together at the centre bottom, knotting the ends too.

Scissor case

Cut a 20 cm square piece of foundation fabric and Pellon. Using the waterproof felt-tip pen, trace the pattern for the front scissor case onto template plastic, and make a window template of the shape. Draw the shape onto the foundation fabric, and baste the Pellon on top. Follow the general directions given above (pages 37–8) to complete the patchwork piece.

Scissor case forms For the scissor case forms, trace the pattern of the front scissor case once, and the back scissor case twice, onto cardboard. To make the front lining, trace the front pattern onto the ultrasuede using a chalk pencil. Cut it out, 1–2 mm *inside* that line. For the back, use one of the back scissor case forms as a template, and trace around it twice with a chalk pencil on the wrong side of the backing/lining fabric. Cut two pieces in this shape, adding a 5 mm seam allowance to the lining piece and a 1 cm allowance to the outer back piece. Cut a piece of Pellon to the exact shape of the back scissor case.

Scissor case back Cover the two forms for the back and back lining with backing/lining fabric, padding the outer form with the piece of Pellon. Fold the seam allowances to the wrong side, and glue them into position. When they are dry, glue the two pieces together, and leave under a weight, such as a heavy book, for an hour or two to ensure that they dry flat and firm. Be sparing with the glue, and avoid getting it on the edges of the shape.

Scissor case front For the front, trim away the foundation fabric and the Pellon to the stitching line of the patchwork piece. Place it over the front template form, turn the seam allowance to the back, and glue in place. Glue the ultrasuede lining to the wrong side of the front scissor case. Lay the piece, face down, on a padded surface and put a weight on top for an hour or two.

Making up Put the two pieces together, right sides out and aligning the edges. Join with a close cretan stitch (see page 18) in a toning colour. If you wish, make a cord 70 cm long (see page 68), and attach and finish in the same manner as for the pincushion.

Fly stitch

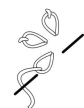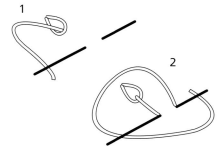

Chain stitch   **Detached chain stitch**

1

2

Zigzag chain stitch

Feathered chain stitch

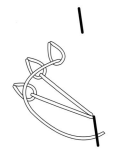

Chequered chain stitch

1   2

Slipped detached chain stitch

Long-tailed chain stitch

Out of this world

THE SUN, THE MOON, the stars and the planets appear on this matching set of bag, purse and spectacles case. In a combination of cottons and silks in the richest of blues, the pieces all showcase patchwork prints with celestial motifs, used as strips in the patchwork, and applied as appliqué motifs. Starry embroidered motifs and star charms continue the theme.

Finished sizes

Bag: 23 × 32 cm
Spectacles case: 16 × 10 cm
Purse: 16 × 13 cm

Materials

50 × 80 cm piece of foundation fabric
50 × 80 cm piece of Pellon
1.7 m of 110 cm wide blue silk for outer bag, purse and case, and lining
1 m of 110 cm wide fusible interfacing
1 m of silky cord (bag handle)
3 m of no. 2 piping cord (bag)
Small pieces of silks or silky fabrics and cottons for patchwork — in blues and starry patterns, including tone-on-tone and mottled prints, and textures
Embroidery threads: silk and cotton stranded and perle threads — particularly in golds, variegated threads, metallics

Small gold beads and sequins
Beading thread
Star and moon charms
Clear snap fasteners (bag and purse, one large, one small)
Navy blue machine sewing thread
Crewel and milliner's needles in a variety of sizes
Pattern-making paper or two A3 sheets of plain photocopy paper
F pencil or Pacer pencil
Waterproof fine-tip felt pen
Chalk pencil
Sheet of template plastic
Quilter's metric ruler
Rotary cutter
Cutting mat

Method

Cut the foundation fabric and Pellon into pieces 45 × 40 cm (bag flap), 15 × 20 cm (purse) and 20 × 30 cm (spectacles case). For the bag, first enlarge the pattern on a photocopier (200 per cent) and make a window template for the bag flap (see page 44). Draw the outline of the flap (the inside edge of the window template) onto the largest piece of foundation fabric. Draw a rectangle on each of the remaining two pieces: 6 × 13 cm for the purse and 16 × 10 cm

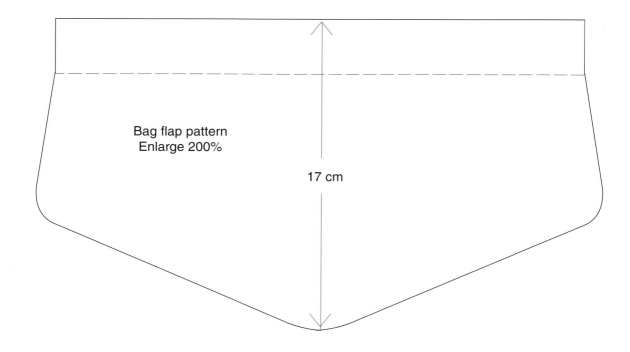

Bag flap pattern
Enlarge 200%

17 cm

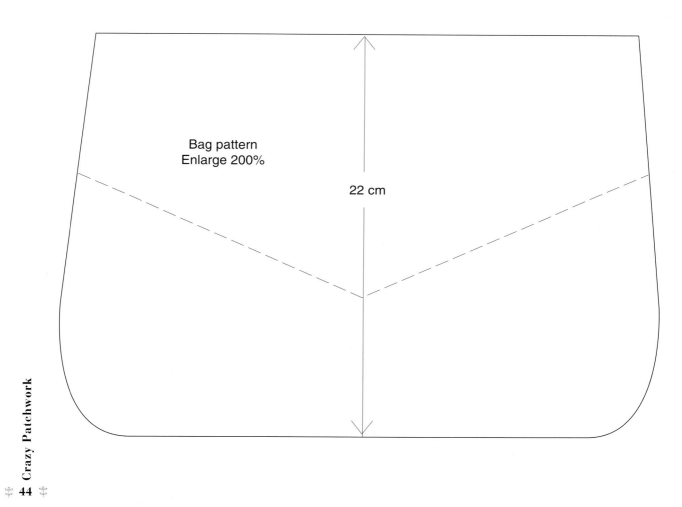

Bag pattern
Enlarge 200%

22 cm

for the spectacles case (you may wish to make window templates for these shapes, too). Baste a piece of Pellon over each piece.

Crazy patchwork Stitch crazy patchwork pieces over each piece, extending beyond the pencilled outline (see *Getting started*, pages 8–9). Use plain and patterned fabrics in a variety of shapes and sizes.

When the patchwork is completed, use the chalk pencil to draw the outline of the bag flap on the top of the patchwork piece, and draw rectangles 6 × 13 cm and 16 × 10 cm (or use window templates if you have made them) on the other two pieces.

Embellishment Embellish the pieces with embroidery, beads and charms. Stitch every seam, and work or apply motifs in the larger areas of plain fabrics.

To secure Renew the chalk outline if necessary on each of the three embroidered pieces. Using the walking foot on the sewing machine and a longer-than-usual stitch, stitch along this line to secure the patches and any embroidery threads that will be cut in the next step. Gently ease the walking foot over beads or thick embroidery.

Using the rotary cutter, cut out each piece, 1 cm from the stitched line. Remove the basting threads.

Preparation Iron the interfacing to 1 m of the blue silk. Cut away the remaining 70 cm piece (called plain silk in the instructions).

Finishing A seam allowance of 1 cm is used throughout, unless otherwise specified. The seam allowance must be added to the bag pattern pieces; it is included in all rotary cut pieces. Always work right sides together, unless otherwise specified.

Stitch notes

Stitch the heads of comets as clusters of french knots in a variety of thread thicknesses, and incorporate some little gold beads. The tails are worked in uneven running stitch, with the stitch on top longer than the stitch below, and with stitches growing longer toward the edges.

Spiral galaxies are worked in stem stitch at the centre, splaying out to uneven running stitch, worked in the same way as for the comets. Stitch a few single gold beads between the lines of stitching on larger galaxies to suggest some more stars. Galaxies can also have french knots at the centre, splaying out to running stitch spirals.

Simple shapes like crescents are worked in stem stitch, with stars worked in straight stitch (see page 14 for more straight stitch stars).

The large crescent and star are silk shapes, attached with paper-backed fusible web (see page 32 for technique) and buttonhole stitch in metallic thread. Use the same method for attaching starry motifs from patchwork fabrics — the back of the spectacles case is plain blue silk with three starry motifs attached in this way.

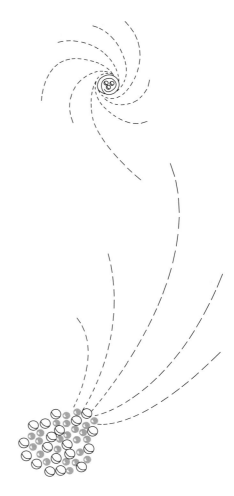

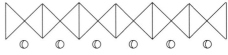

Bag

Make paper patterns of the bag flap and the bag body (page 44); note that pattern pieces do *not* include seam allowances.

Cutting From the interfaced fabric cut two strips 6 × 76 cm for the gusset and gusset lining (this measurement *includes* a 1 cm seam allowance on each long side and a 2 cm turn-in at each end).

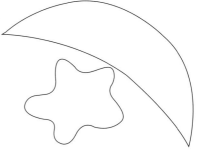

Out of this world

Special prints like the starry ones used here can add a delightful dimension to crazy patchwork. However, it's perilously easy to go overboard, trying to include *everything* you have collected, and ending up with a very crowded piece of patchwork. Make sure that you incorporate plenty of plain, tone-on-tone or mottled patterns to give you space for ample embroidery.

Using the enlarged pattern piece for the bag body, cut three bag shapes from interfaced fabric for the front, front lining, and back, adding a 1 cm seam allowance on every side.

To make the lining for the back and flap, join the paper patterns for the bag back and bag flap, aligning the cut edges of the straight edges. Cut a single piece in interfaced fabric in this shape for the back bag and flap. Use a short chalk line or stitch to mark the fabric where the top of the bag back joins the flap.

Join the patchwork bag flap to the bag back along the straight edge.

Piping From the 70 cm piece of plain silk fabric, cut bias strips 3 cm wide from the blue silk fabric, and join them together to make a strip 3 m long. Use this strip and the piping cord to make piping (see page 68).

Pin the piping to the right side of the bag back–flap piece, matching the raw edges. Start and finish along the bottom edge away from a corner. Clip the binding a little on the curves and ease it round, so that it will not be tight when the bag is finished.

Using the zipper foot on the sewing machine, attach the piping to the back–flap piece, using the standard stitch size and stitching as closely as possible to the piping. Overlap the piping at the start and finish, taking the ends into the seam allowance; cutting away the piping cord from inside the fabric of one end helps keep this overlap flat.

Fold in the 1 cm seam allowance along the top straight edge of the bag front. Attach piping to the front bag piece in the same manner as for the back–flap piece, but start and end at the top edges (the top straight edge of the bag front is not piped). Leave about 2–3 cm of piping at each end to fold to the wrong side.

Gussets Fold in 2 cm at the two short ends of the outer bag gusset strip. Stitch the gusset to the side and bottom edges of the piped bag front. Use the zipper foot in order to stitch closely to the piping cord.

Stitch the bag back to the other side of the gusset, matching the top edge of the gusset strip with the chalk mark on the bag back.

Stitch the lining together in the same manner as the bag, omitting the piping.

Assembly Leave both the bag and the bag lining wrong sides out. Pin the patchwork flap to the flap lining, right sides together. Stitch around the sides and curved edge of the flap, stitching as closely as possible to the piping cord (use the zipper foot). Trim the corners and clip the curves. Trim away as much of the Pellon and foundation fabric as possible.

Turn the flap through to the right side. Finger-press the seam (see page 22). Turn the outer bag through to the right side, and push the lining inside it.

Align the folded edges of the front bag and front lining, and gusset and gusset lining. Pin the front edge. Push the edges of the cord between the gusset and the gusset lining, and pin and stitch firmly in place. Stitch the gussets and bag top together by hand or machine.

Attach a snap fastener to the back of the flap and the bag, or attach a button to the bag just below the point of the flap, and stitch a buttonhole loop (see page 6) to the flap.

Out of this world describes the stars, comets, galaxies and
moons decorating this set of bag, purse and spectacles case
in celestial blues and rich golds (page 43).

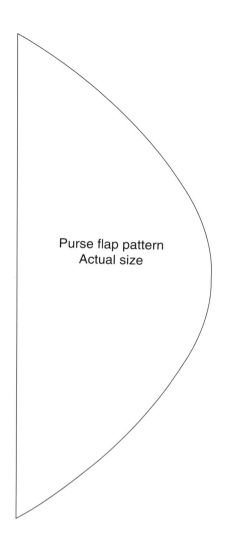

Purse flap pattern
Actual size

Purse

Make a paper pattern of the purse flap (on this page).

Cutting From the interfaced silk, and using a rotary cutter, cut rectangles measuring 27 × 15 cm (for the bottom edge, back and flap of the purse, called the back in the following instructions) and 9 × 15 cm (the top piece of the purse, lying under the flap).

From the plain silk, cut a strip measuring 41 × 15 cm for the lining. These measurements all include 1 cm seam allowances.

Turn in 1 cm along one long edge of the top piece to the wrong side. Stitch the other long edge to the top edge of the patchwork piece. Stitch the back piece to the opposite edge of the patchwork piece. Press a fold in the back piece 3 cm from the patchwork piece to form the bottom edge of the purse. Turn to the wrong side, and stitch the side seams up to the edge of the fold of the top piece (16 cm). Clip the corners and grade the seam allowances, trimming away as much as possible of the Pellon and foundation fabric.

Lining Turn in 1 cm along one short edge of the lining. Press a fold on the wrong side 16 cm from the folded edge to form the base of the lining. Stitch the side seams up to the folded edge at the top of the purse. Grade the seam allowances and clip the corners.

Assembly With the wrong sides of the purse and lining facing out, pin the flaps right sides together. Pin the flap pattern to the fabric, aligning the straight edge with the top edge of the purse. Stitch the flaps together around the edge of the pattern. Clip the curve and grade the seam allowances. Turn the flap to the right side, and finger-press (see page 22).

Turn the purse to the right side, and push the lining inside it. Align the two folded edges at the top and stitch closed by hand or machine.

Attach a clear snap fastener to the body and flap of the purse.

Spectacles case

From the interfaced fabric, cut a rectangle 18 × 12 cm for the back of the case. From the plain silk, cut two rectangles 18 × 12 cm for the lining, and a 30 cm bias strip 3.5 cm wide. Cut a piece of Pellon 18 × 12 cm.

To join case and lining Place the patchwork front and the interfaced back piece right sides together. Against the wrong side of the back, place the piece of Pellon, then the two pieces of lining fabric on top of the Pellon. Stitch around the side and bottom edges of the fabric stack. Clip the corners and grade the seam allowances. From the patchwork piece, trim away as much as possible of the Pellon and foundation fabric.

Bias edging Turn the case right side out. Stitch the bias strip around the top edge of the case, overlapping the edges, making sure a lining piece lies against both the front and back pieces of the case. Trim the seam allowance to 5 mm. Turn the strip to the wrong side of the case, turn the case wrong side out, turn in the raw edge of the binding, and stitch in place.

Precious jewels

MAKE A COLLECTION of precious jewels in crazy patchwork. Great fun and quick to make, these brooches use the tiniest scraps of fabric, and the most brilliant of threads, beads, 'jewels' and charms. Make some patchwork pieces from the scraps whenever you make a crazy project, and complete them when you need a gift for someone.

Finished sizes

Circle: 6 cm in diameter
Triangle: 6.5 cm high
Small heart: 6 cm at its widest
Large heart: 7 cm at its widest
Oval: 6 cm at its widest

Long heart: 8 cm high
Long teardrop: 6.5 cm high
Wide teardrop: 5.5 cm high
Long narrow oval: 8.5 cm long

Materials

12 cm square of foundation fabric for each brooch
12–16 cm square of Pellon, for each brooch
10 cm square of ultrasuede for backing (this is generally a generous amount for the backing, but if you are going to make several brooches, it is most economical to buy a 15 cm strip of ultrasuede)
Small pieces of silks or silky fabrics for patchwork
Embroidery threads: silk and cotton stranded and perle threads, and variegated threads, metallics and synthetics to suit your colour scheme
Silk ribbon
Small lace motifs or scraps of lace
Small beads and sequins

Beading thread
Charms
Sew-on craft 'jewels', or cabochons
Crewel, milliner's, sharps and chenille needles in a variety of sizes
Machine sewing thread — ecru for light, grey for darker fabrics
Brooch pins
Clear-drying craft glue, such as 450 adhesive
Hot glue gun or beading thread for attaching pins to brooches
F pencil or Pacer pencil
Waterproof fine-tip felt pen
Chalk pencil
Sheet of template plastic
Template plastic or firm cardboard for brooch forms

Method

Use the permanent marker to trace the brooch shape you want onto template plastic. Cut out the shape and draw around it on the foundation fabric with pencil. Note that the brooches are made directly on

CRAZY WISDOM

Whenever you are making a small piece of crazy patchwork, or a piece that is to be turned over a firm shape, like these brooches, keep the number of patches to a minimum. Three, or at most four, pieces applied to the foundation will give you a simple edge to work with when it comes to finishing the piece, and good spaces to decorate with stitchery and beadwork. It is also important to make sure that seam lines do not cross points or notches (as in the hearts), as this extra thickness will cause problems in making up the brooches.

Make *Precious jewels* from scraps of fabric and decorate with beads, jewels and brilliant threads. The circle is 6 cm in diameter (page 49).

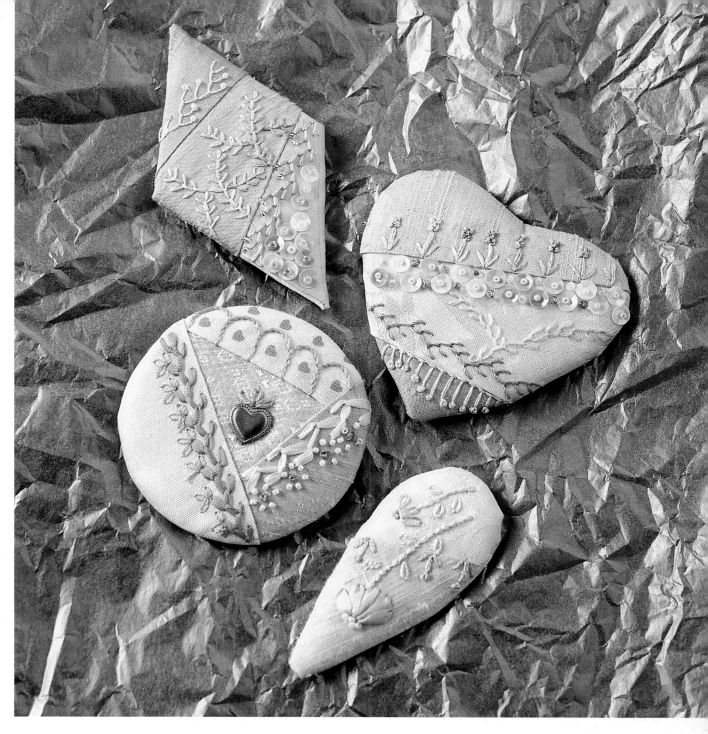

the foundation fabric with no Pellon; the Pellon listed is used for padding the brooch itself.

Crazy patchwork Stitch crazy patchwork pieces on the foundation fabric, extending beyond the pencilled outline (see *Getting started*, pages 8–9). Use plain and patterned fabrics in a variety of shapes and sizes. Include plain fabrics to give space for embroidery.

When the patchwork is completed, use the template and a chalk pencil to draw an outline of the final shape onto the patchwork.

Embellishment Embellish the patchwork piece with embroidery, beads and charms. Stitch every seam, and work motifs in the larger

Pastel colours, sequins and beads, and ribbon embroidery make delicate *Precious jewels* (page 49).

Brooch templates, actual size

areas of plain fabrics. Do not add any beads or thick threads beyond the outline, and do all finishing off inside the final shape.

To finish

When the embroidery is completed, redraw the chalk outline if necessary. Work a small running stitch over this outline, starting and ending the stitching on the right side of the piece. Cut out the piece 1 cm past the stitching line. Trim the foundation fabric right up to the stitching line.

Preparation Cut two or three pieces of Pellon to pad the brooch: cut the first one, which will go directly behind the fabric, the same size as the template, the second 1–2 mm smaller than that, and the third, 1–2 mm smaller than the second, centring these two on top of the first piece, with the smallest piece uppermost.

Cut the brooch shape in template plastic or cardboard for the brooch form; if the plastic is very thin, cut two pieces and join with a dab of glue. Put the form on top of the stack of Pellon (the form sits on top of the smallest piece of Pellon). For the brooch back, cut a piece of ultrasuede 1–2 mm smaller than the template.

Circle, oval and teardrop shapes For the circle, oval and teardrop brooches, start with a firm double stitch, and work a small running stitch in the seam allowance of the brooches, about 3 mm from the stitching line, but do not finish off the thread.

Put the stack of Pellon and the brooch form on the back of the patchwork piece, ensuring that it is centred. Pull up the gathering thread so that the patchwork is drawn taut over the padded form. Finish off the thread.

Dab a little craft glue under the seam allowance (a match is helpful here), and flatten the gathered fabric as much as possible. Apply craft glue to the ultrasuede, and glue it to the back of the brooch. If you do not have a hot glue gun (see *Finishing* below), attach the brooch pin (you will need the kind with small holes along the bar) to the ultrasuede before gluing the backing to the brooch. Use beading thread and a few straight stitches into each hole.

Place the brooch face down on a well-padded surface with a weight, such as a heavy book, on top for an hour or two to ensure that the brooch dries flat and straight. Put a weight on each side of the pin if it has been sewn in place.

Other shapes All the other shapes are finished with glue only, and omit the gathering stitch. Turn the seam allowance on these shapes to the wrong side of the brooch form, turning in the corners first, and glue the points, then the edges, to the form. On curves, such as the top of the heart, it is best to clip the notch and the curve, so that the fabric will sit flatter — but don't clip too energetically, because you do not want to see cut edges around the edges of the brooch back. Glue the ultrasuede to the back in the same manner as for the rounded shapes, and weight the piece while it dries. If you don't have a hot glue gun, sew the pins in place as described for the circle shape above.

Finishing Finally, remove the line of running stitches marking the edge of the brooch shape, and use the hot glue gun to glue the brooch pin to the back of the brooch, placing it in the upper part of the shape so that the brooch will sit well when worn.

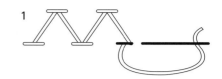

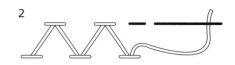

Chevron stitch

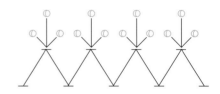

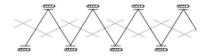

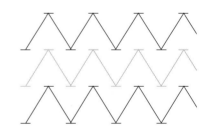

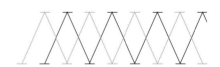

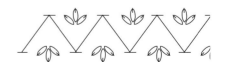

The realms of gold

MAKE AN EXQUISITE crazy patchwork cushion cover in the richest of gold and cream fabrics. The frame of gold fabric, which extends in a flange around the cushion, highlights the patchwork, laces, ribbon and embroidery. It would make an elegant cushion for the bedroom, teamed with the sachets in matching colours. Shadow work bows and ribbon embroidery add new dimensions.

Finished sizes

Cushion: 45 cm square (59 cm square with flange)
Sachet: 10 cm square

Materials

40 cm of 110 cm wide foundation fabric (enough for one cushion cover and six sachets)

60 cm of 90 cm wide Pellon (enough for one cushion cover and six sachets, and sachet backs)

1.4 m of 110 cm wide plain gold fabric for borders and backing (cushion cover)

15 cm of 110 cm wide plain silk for backing (enough for nine sachets)

70 cm of fine cord for each sachet, or a skein of no. 5 perle thread (to make a twisted cord) in gold or cream

10–15 cm square of silk organza for each shadow work motif

Small pieces of silks or silky fabrics for patchwork — in creams and golds, in patterns, embroidered fabrics, plains and tone-on-tone prints, and textures — and patchwork cottons in creams with lacy or tone-on-tone patterns

Embroidery threads: silk and cotton stranded and perle threads — in golds and creams,

variegated stranded threads, synthetics, metallics

Silk ribbon in a variety of widths — in golds and creams

Small beads — in gold

Beading thread

Scraps of braids, ribbons, silk ribbon — in gold and cream

Scraps of lace and lace motifs

Gold charms (optional)

Lavender or potpourri (sachets)

Mother-of-pearl or shell buttons

35 cm pale gold zip to match backing fabric

45 cm cushion insert

Ecru machine sewing thread

Gold-coloured machine sewing thread (to finish cushion cover)

Crewel, milliner's, sharps and chenille needles in a variety of sizes

Blue water-erasable marking pen

F pencil or Pacer pencil

Waterproof fine-tip felt pen

Chalk pencil

Sheet of template plastic

Quilter's metric ruler

Rotary cutter

Cutting mat

Shadow work method

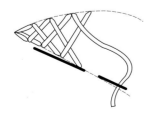

A collection of cream and gold fabrics, painted lace, delicate shadow embroidery and a multitude of stitches and beads on sachets and a cushion make up *The realms of gold* collection (page 54).

Method

Make a 27 cm square window template for the cushion and a 10 cm square window template for the sachets (see page 12).

For the cushion, cut a 40 cm square of foundation fabric, and use pencil to draw a 27 cm square on it. For each sachet, cut a 20 cm square of foundation fabric and use pencil to draw a 10 cm square on it. Baste a same-size piece of Pellon over each foundation piece.

Crazy patchwork For the cushion and the sachets, stitch crazy patchwork pieces over each piece, extending beyond the pencilled outline (see *Getting started*, page 8–9). Use plain and patterned fabrics in a variety of shapes and sizes. Include plenty of plain or almost-plain fabrics to give space for embroidery. Incorporate laces, ribbons and braids as you work, so that their raw edges can be sewn into the next seam.

Embellishment When the patchwork is completed, use the window template and a chalk pencil to draw an outline of the shape of the cushion or sachet onto the patchwork. Embellish the patchwork piece with embroidery, beads, lace, ribbon and charms. Stitch every seam, and work or apply motifs in the larger areas of plain fabrics.

To secure When the embroidery is completed, redraw the chalk outline on the patchwork if necessary. Using the walking foot on the sewing machine and a longer-than-usual stitch, stitch along this line to secure the patches and any embroidery threads that will be cut in the next step. Cut out each piece 1 cm past the stitching line. Remove the basting threads.

Stitch notes

Shadow work motifs have been featured on the cushion and sachets. Make the shadow work motifs on organza, cut them out with a wide area around them, and baste to a cream-coloured satin-finish silk. You can then incorporate them in the patchwork just as you do any other patch.

To do the embroidery, first trace the pattern onto organza using the water-erasable pen. Working from the back of the piece, stitch in closed herringbone stitch (see the diagram on page 54), working each stitch into the hole created by the previous stitch — on the right side of the work, it has the appearance of backstitch. When you can no longer work across the space, complete lines with stem stitch worked from the back, which will again produce the effect of backstitch on the front. I worked these motifs in one strand of stranded silk thread. The little points on the Tudor rose were worked in a single fly stitch with a tiny tail in a single strand of metallic thread.

When the embroidery is complete, hold the piece of embroidery under a cold tap and allow plenty of cold water to flow through to remove all trace of the pen. Dry and press. Do not press the piece dry as this can make any residue of the pen marks reappear.

Cushion

A 1 cm seam allowance is used throughout. Always work with right sides together, unless otherwise specified.

Borders Cut four strips of gold silk measuring 18 × 80 cm for the borders and flanges (includes a 1 cm seam allowance). Add the borders, mitring the corners (see page 69).

Cushion back Cut two pieces of gold silk measuring 32 × 61 cm (includes 1 cm seam allowances, with a 1.5 cm seam allowance at the centre). Matching the raw edges, stitch the two pieces together for 8 cm at each end along the 61 cm edge, using a 1.5 cm seam allowance (61 cm square of fabric). Press the seam allowances open. Insert a zip in the opening at the centre back.

Assembly Open the zip, and stitch the cushion back to the front around all four sides. Turn to the right side and use the chalk pencil to mark a 45 cm square, centred on the pillow top, pinning the top and back together so that they don't slip.

Machine stitch in gold-coloured thread along this line, to define the separation between the cushion shape and the flange. Insert the pillow form.

Sachets

For each sachet, cut a 12 cm square piece of backing silk and a 12 cm square of Pellon (includes 1 cm seam allowance). Stitch the patchwork and the backing fabric together, with the Pellon against the wrong side of the backing. Leave a 4 cm opening for turning, ensuring all the corners are stitched.

Turn through, fill with lavender or potpourri, and stitch the opening closed by hand.

Attach a ribbon tie at one corner for hanging the sachet, or use whipstitch to attach a cord around the edge of the sachet, incorporating a loop for hanging the sachet if required. If you want to use a twisted cord in perle thread, see page 68 for instructions on how to make it.

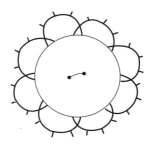

Button on lace

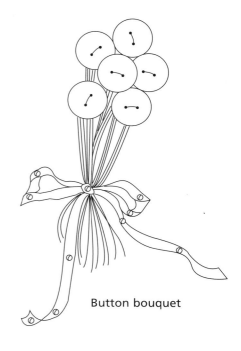

Button bouquet

Button flowers

Create a bunch of flowers with little buttons, or make a new row of them with straight stitch stems and detached button hole leaves, or centre a large button on a scrap of lace.

Gentle hearts

THE MOST DELICATE of pink, silver and cream fabrics are formed into heart shapes, which are then appliquéd to pink silk patches — a special method is used to make appliquéing the crazy patchwork hearts as simple as can be. This romantic wall hanging is the perfect opportunity to use the most extravagant embroidery, beading and ribbon work that you could want. If pink is not to your liking, try other pastels or jewel tones on black for a brilliant look.

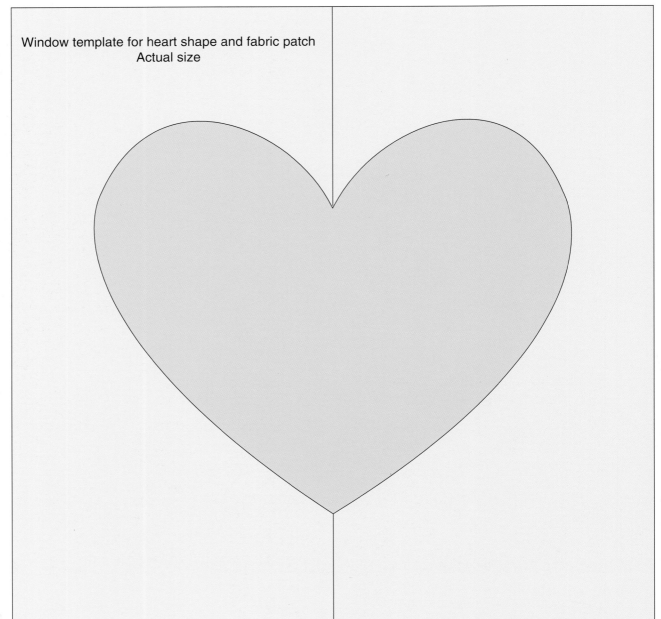

Window template for heart shape and fabric patch
Actual size

The most delicate of pink hearts, richly decorated with stitches, laces, ribbons and all kinds of beads, buttons and charms, make the *Dear hearts* wall hanging (page 58).

Finished size

59 cm square

Materials

30 cm of 115 cm wide foundation fabric	Beading thread
30 cm of 90 cm wide Pellon	Charms
30 cm of 115 cm wide voile or organza	Shell and mother-of-pearl buttons and shapes
1.6 m of 115 cm wide medium-weight plain silk, such as Thai or dupion, for background, border, backing and binding	Small buttons
	Pink machine sewing thread to match background fabric
	Light-coloured thread for basting or safety pins
70 cm square piece of batting	Pink quilting thread
Small pieces of silks or silky fabrics, laces and cottons for patchwork — in pinks, silver, greys and creams; in textures, patterns and plain	16 pink, shell or mother-of-pearl buttons, about 12 mm in diameter
	Anti-fray product, such as Fray Stoppa (optional)
Embroidery threads: silk and cotton stranded and perle threads, variegated threads, silver metallic threads	Crewel, milliner's, sharps and chenille needles in a variety of sizes
	Betweens needle size 8–12 for quilting
Scraps of lace and lace motifs	F pencil or Pacer pencil
Small pieces of ribbons and light braids	Waterproof fine-tip felt pen
	Chalk pencil
Silk ribbon for embroidery and attached bows	18 cm square piece of template plastic
Small beads, including fancy shapes and bugle beads — in pink, crystal and silver	Quilter's metric ruler
	Rotary cutter
	Cutting mat

Method

Use the template plastic and the waterproof pen to make a window template (see page 12), tracing the heart and patch shape on page 58, and including the centre line.

The inner line is the final shape of the heart, and the outer line is the 17 cm square to be cut for the patch each heart is attached to. Use the interior line for marking the heart shape on the foundation fabric, the patchwork piece and the voile or organza used to back the heart. Use the outer line to mark the 17 cm cutting line for the patches, if you are not using a rotary cutter. To ensure that each heart is precisely positioned, place the window template over the 17 cm square patch, set the heart into the window, and pin it in place. It's very important, with a single repeat pattern like this, that every piece is placed in exactly the same position on its background patch, which the window template helps you to do.

For each of the nine hearts, cut a 15 cm piece of foundation fabric and Pellon. Using the window template, draw a pencil outline of the heart onto each piece of the foundation fabric. Baste a piece of Pellon over each piece.

Crazy patchwork Stitch crazy patchwork pieces over the foundation in the usual manner, extending beyond the pencilled outline (see *Getting started*, pages 8–9). Use plain, textured and patterned fabrics in a variety of shapes and sizes. Incorporate lace, ribbon and braids as you work, so that their raw edges can be sewn into the next seam. Add any additional pieces of lace, ribbon or braid, extending into seam allowance on each side. Attach with a decorative stitch.

The hearts Cut nine 13 cm square pieces of voile or organza. Use the template and pencil to trace the heart outline onto each piece of interfacing.

Place a piece of voile or organza, pencil side up, over the right side of a patchwork heart, aligning it to make the most of the fabrics, and ensuring that the patchwork seams do not fall near the point or the notch at the top.

Machine-stitch right around the heart, using a small stitch, and stitching slowly around the curves at the top of the heart. Grade the seam allowance, trimming the point, cutting deep into the notch, and clipping a few times around the curves at the top. Cut away most of the foundation fabric and the Pellon.

Carefully lift the voile or organza away from the patchwork piece, and make a small cut in the centre of the voile or organza. Enlarge the cut vertically towards the top and bottom of the heart, and cut diagonally from the centre towards the tops of the curves. Make sure you keep a good 2 cm away from the seams.

Gently turn the heart right side out, pulling the point or one of the curves through first. Finger-press (see page 22). If any stitches are visible at the notch, cut them very carefully with snips or sharp-pointed embroidery scissors, and remove the threads. Gently press the hearts if you wish, placing them face down on a well-padded surface, such as a stack of towelling on the ironing board.

Embellishment Embellish the hearts with embroidery, beads, buttons, lace motifs, ribbon pieces and charms. Stitch every seam, and work or apply motifs or bead patterns or silk ribbon bows in the larger areas of plain fabrics.

Stitch notes

The two bows are made with silk ribbon, tied and twisted or folded into position, then secured in place with french knots or beads.

Flowers are worked in silk ribbon. The single one is made of soft straight stitches, with beads at the top to represent the centre. Leaves are tiny straight stitches. The cluster of flowers is made with french knots in ribbon, with tiny thread knots in the centre of each. The leaves are worked in stranded cotton in detached chain. Both stems are worked in stem stitch. Stem stitch is used for the heart shapes.

The spider's web, worked in silver metallic thread, fills a single patch. The spokes are long straight stitches, unevenly spaced. Work the rounds in straight stitch from spoke to spoke. Bringing the needle up on the right-hand side of the first spoke, take the needle over the spoke, go through to the back of the fabric immediately alongside the further edge of the next spoke, and come up immediately alongside the other side of the second spoke (making the tiniest of backstitches). Finally, take the thread over the next spoke. Repeat all around the web. Don't try to fill the whole space with rings: the web looks better with bare spokes at the edges.

CRAZY WISDOM Sometimes, when all the patchwork is complete, and you are happily embellishing your work, a ghastly sight appears — frayed edges or even little gaps between the fabrics where the Pellon or foundation fabric peeks through! Don't despair. Carefully trim away any fluff or threads and stitch a piece of braid, a lace motif, a button or a cluster of buttons and charms over the offending spot. No one will ever know.

Herringbone stitch

Laced herringbone stitch

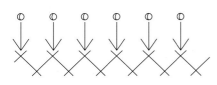

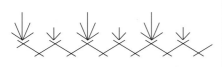

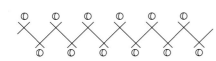

The spider is made with two tiny satin stitch dots, each stitch worked in and out of the same two holes for each dot. The eyes are french knots, and the legs are straight stitches.

To finish

A seam allowance of 1 cm is used throughout. Always sew with right sides together, unless otherwise specified.

Cutting For the border pieces, cut four 6 cm wide strips across the width of the fabric. For the binding, cut three 6 cm wide strips across the width of the fabric; join them to make a strip 3 m long.

Cut nine 17 cm squares of background silk, using the window template or the rotary cutter and ruler. Use the window template to place a heart in the centre of each patch, lining up the point and the notch with the centre lines. Pin or baste the heart in position, and use pink thread and a tiny appliqué stitch (see page 6) to attach each one to its background square.

Construction Set out the nine blocks in your preferred arrangement. Stitch each row of three blocks together, using a 1 cm seam allowance. Then join the three rows together.

Add the borders, mitring the corners (see page 69).

Basting Cut a piece of backing fabric measuring 70 cm square, and press to ensure that it is wrinkle free. Lay it out, wrong side up, on a work table, and use masking tape to hold it in position, making sure that the fabric is straight and taut, but not stretched or distorted.

Lay the piece of batting on top. Lay the completed patchwork on top of this, and centre it over the bottom pieces. Secure the top to the table, but don't pull it too tight. Baste or pin the three layers together, starting at the centre.

Quilting Starting with the centre heart, quilt in the ditch around each heart. Stitch a button at the intersection of every block and at the points where block intersections meet the border, working through all three layers. Remove the pins as you work towards the edge, but leave the outer row in place until the binding is pinned in place. Remove all the basting after the binding is attached.

Use the rotary cutter and quilter's ruler to trim the backing and batting level with the raw edges of the quilt.

Rod pocket Cut a strip of backing fabric 8 cm wide and 60 cm long to make a rod pocket for the hanging (use an anti-fray product on the short ends of the silk if you wish). Turn in 5 cm at each short end of the strip, and fold it in half along its length, right sides out. Place the raw edges of the pocket against the raw edge at the top of the back of the quilt. It will be stitched in place with the binding.

Binding Fold the binding strip in half along its length, right sides out, to make a double binding 3 cm wide. Press. Pin the binding around the edges of the quilt on the right side, matching the raw edges, and stitch all the layers together 1 cm from the edge, mitring the corners (see page 69). When you have stitched the binding in place, join the two ends of the binding together. Turn the folded edge of the binding to the wrong side, and hem in place along the line of stitching.

Stitch the rod pocket to the back of the quilt, about 1 cm from the pocket fold.

Techniques and technicalities

GETTING STARTED (pages 7–12) showed you how to prepare the patchwork base for crazy patchwork. Once this piece is finished, the fun really starts with the embellishment — using embroidery, appliqué, ribbon, laces, beads, buttons and charms. This section describes the techniques and equipment you will use to embellish and make up your projects.

Some of the best embroidery stitches for crazy patchwork are illustrated throughout the book, both with diagrams to show how to work them and sketches showing how to use and combine them (the *Index* will help you find them.) Where straight lines appear in these sketches, use stem, chain or backstitch, as you prefer. Where little knots, circles or beads are shown, you can stitch a bead or work a colonial knot or a french knot (see pages 5 and 13). Long 'corkscrews' represent bullion stitches (see page 53).

The stitches included here offer plenty of variety, and they are all easily mastered, but you will soon want more. A list of the best stitch books is included under *Useful books* on page 70.

Embellishment

About the only rule that exists in crazy patchwork is that every seam line must be embroidered. Originally, this embroidery secured every fabric piece in place, but with the piecing now done on the machine, the embroidery has become purely decorative. Use as few or as many stitches as you like — it can be fun to restrict yourself to one stitch and use only variations of it for a whole piece.

Large plain spaces can be filled with embroidered motifs worked directly onto the surface. Specially worked embroidery, such as the shadow stitched bows in *The realms of gold* (pages 54–7), can be incorporated like any other fabric patches. Purchased embroidered motifs can be included, and so can lace motifs, bits of tatting, ribbon, ribbon bows and rosettes, and appliqué motifs. Fancy threads, such as chenille and bouclé, and thick threads, as well as ribbons, can be trailed over the surface and couched into place.

Some people say a spider's web should appear on every piece, but sometimes this just wouldn't suit the piece; and if you do a lot of crazy patchwork it could get plain boring. If anyone tells you

CRAZY WISDOM

Don't pick — or unpick! It is easy to set off in pursuit of perfection when you are sewing (especially if the Stitch Police are watching; see page 5). This can lead to all sorts of trouble — worrying away at your work, pulling it and rubbing it in the belief that you can make it just right if you pat it enough. Don't do it! All that will happen if you continually redo your work is that you will make it grubby, and make stitches flat or distorted and threads fluffy. Continual unpicking will make your work look worse, not better: you will leave needle marks in the fabric, as well as tiny marks and bits of fluff from the thread as it becomes harder and harder to remove. And above all it's boring and unproductive. Instead of whipping up a couple of brooches in an afternoon you will end up with more UFOs for the bottom drawer, and make yourself unhappy.

Remember, this is supposed to be fun! No one will see every tiny imperfection when your project is finished — the impression comes from the look of the whole piece, not every tiny stitch. And if you do have Stitch Police among your friends and relatives, ignore what they say, or deprive them of the chance to see, or receive, your work.

Simply do the best you can — and your best will vary depending on things like how you are feeling, all the other demands on your time, and when you are stitching. Make sure you have the best lighting, materials and equipment you can manage. And keep a couple of projects on the go at once, so there is something to do on wobbly-hand or tired-eyes days, and something exquisite to do when everything around you is perfect.

that you must have a spider's web, ignore them. However, some people think spiders and spider's webs are lucky, so if you want to include them, do.

In embellishing your patchwork you will discover the versatility of crazy patchwork, because you can use every style of embroidery, and show off all your special skills.

Ribbon embroidery particularly suits some pieces. You can also use ribbon to divide patches that are too big, to obscure untidy bits, to decorate a seam, to trail over the surface in a meandering pattern, and to tie bows and attach them with stitches or beads. Use decorative stitches or beads to attach ribbons or pieces of lace, to the patchwork, rather than an invisible appliqué stitch.

Beads can be used to embellish stitches further, at the tips of feather stitch, for instance; to pick out details in lace or in a patterned fabric; or to create new patterns over the surface of the fabric. Add beads after the rest of the embroidery is done so that your working threads don't catch on them.

Charms can contribute to the theme of a piece, or simply add new and interesting shapes. Buttons can also be used alone, sitting on lace motifs or ribbon rosettes, or made into little groupings. Add both of these when all the rest of the embellishment is complete, or your working threads will catch on them. Attach them with decorative threads and decorative stitches. Keep these to a minimum in pieces that will be used a lot, such as the bag and purse in *Out of this world* (pages 43–8).

Crazy patchwork can be as wild or as restrained as you want it to be.

Threads

Every kind of thread you can find can be used in crazy — if it's too difficult to sew with, it can be couched (see page 6) onto the surface as bows or trails, or in any decorative pattern you fancy. The variety of threads available today is a great temptation to the crazy patchworker, but you can get by with just a few. If you have spent all your craft budget on gorgeous fabrics, you could survive (for a while, anyway!) with just DMC stranded cotton number 729, which is a beautiful gold colour. And the freedom of crazy patchwork means that you can use what you have on hand, including all the leftovers from kits and other projects: you don't need to know the colour number or even the brand — if it matches the project colours, use it!

Stranded cottons are readily available in craft and sewing shops, but fancy threads, variegated threads, silks and the full range of perle threads are available only from specialised embroidery shops (those listed on pages 71–2 will supply you by mail order). Craft shows are the perfect chance to find new threads.

Stranded cottons made by DMC, Madeira, Anchor and Semco are all readily available. You can use all three brands in the one project, so that you can choose the colours that will work best. In addition, many varieties of over-dyed or variegated threads are now available, including those made by Minnamurra Threads in Australia and from American companies such as Needle Necessities. Two strands of stranded cotton were generally used in projects in this book, though you should use the number of strands that will produce the effect you want. Heavyweight fabrics or strong patterns will need more strands to create an impact. For knotted stitches, such as french and colonial knots, use up to six strands for really full and dramatic stitches.

Perle cottons, also known as pearl cottons, have more sheen than stranded cottons, and are available in various thicknesses: the finer ones (higher numbers) are easy to sew with, and the thicker ones give more dramatic effects. These threads are not separated into strands. Use number 5 perle cotton for tassels and cords. Variegated perle cottons are made by Minnamurra and Kacoonda in Australia, and Caron in America (this company calls its perle thread Watercolours; it is sometimes presented with three of the individual strands lightly twisted together so that they can easily be separated).

Soft cottons are fine threads — including Wildflowers by Caron, and Danish Flower Thread — that are particularly attractive in country-look projects. The single strands — equal to about the thickness of two or three strands of stranded thread — are used alone, or two can be used together for a stronger effect.

Stranded silks are separated into individual strands, just like stranded cottons. Depending on the brand, stranded silks are made up of four to twelve strands. They are slightly thicker than stranded cottons, and a single strand is perfect for projects such as *Victorian tiles* (pages 28–34). As with stranded cottons, however, you can simply increase the number of strands being used to get a stronger or more dramatic effect. The most common brands available are Au ver à soie and Madeira. In addition, there are some variegated types available, the most beautiful being Waterlilies by Caron, and they have been much used in these projects.

Perle silks vary in thickness, like the cottons. Au ver à soie's Soie Gobelins is a fine thread that has been used in nearly all of these projects, though the

Single feather stitch

Feather stitch

Double feather stitch

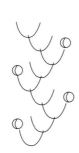

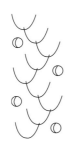

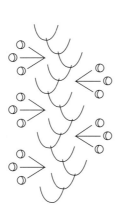

Straight feather stitch

1

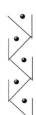

2

Double straight feather stitch

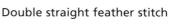

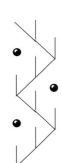

Closed feather stitch

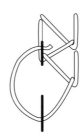

Techniques and technicalities

company also produces a thicker thread, Soie Perlée, which is perfect for larger and more dramatic stitches. Gumnut Yarns and Kacoonda produce variegated perle silks. Kanagawa and YLI silks are also available in a huge range of colours.

Synthetics include the brilliantly sheened rayon Brazilian embroidery threads, which are perle-style threads, and the stranded threads, Marlitt from DMC, and Decora by Madeira. These threads may be a little trickier to sew with than the silk and cotton threads, and if you find them so, work with shorter lengths than usual. America's Rainbow Gallery also produces synthetic perle threads, one of which is Patina perle rayon.

Fancy threads also seem to increase every year. Bouclé, in variegated skeins, and chenille threads (in both plain and variegated skeins) are particularly useful for special effects or for tied bows or couched trails, though neither is easy to sew with. Charleston by Needle Necessities is a surprising long-haired sparkly yarn made of polyamide. If you sew with fancy threads, use big-eyed needles, so that the thread doesn't get worn being pulled through the fabric, and short lengths. Rainbow Gallery also makes many ribbons and ribbon-like threads. Caron also produces synthetic tubular ribbons to be used as threads. Fascinating threads and ribbons appear in thread packages produced by Perri's Threads and Sanshi. Cotton On Creations in Australia also makes colour co-ordinated packages of a variety of threads and ribbons (Thread Packs).

Metallics add a special lustre to crazy patchwork. Many different kinds are available — from Madeira, DMC, Kreinik and Au ver à soie — but one that is very easy to use is Madeira's Metallic Effect Yarn for Embroidery and Knitting, which is a stranded thread. A thin metallic yarn can also be combined with one or two strands of stranded cotton or silk for a different effect and easier working. Use them to highlight or whip other stitches, as well as trying the full range of embroidery stitches with them.

Ribbon work and ribbon embroidery

Ribbon can be tied into bows and attached to crazy patchwork with stitches or with beads. It can be twisted and trailed, and couched into place (see page 6). Narrow double-sided polyester can be used for stitchery or for bows. Use wide double-sided polyester ribbon for larger effects, such as rosettes, to be sewn to the patchwork.

Silk ribbon, which is particularly malleable, can be used for ribbon embroidery with stunning effect in crazy patchwork. Many colours are available in silk, including variegated ones, produced by Kacoonda in Australia and by Petals in America. Several widths are also available. Spark organdie ribbon can add a bright effect, used in the same way as silk ribbon.

Only very simple stitches have been used for the ribbon embroidery in this book: straight and chain stitches, and french knots — all made in exactly the same manner as stitches worked in thread. Use a chenille needle and fix the ribbon before you start work. To do this, pull about 5 cm of ribbon through the needle's eye. Pierce this short end with the point of the needle, and gently pull the long end of thread near the needle's eye to pull the short end of the thread around the eye. Start and end silk ribbon embroidery by leaving short tails on the wrong side of the work and stitching them in place with embroidery or machine thread.

Always make silk ribbon stitches sit softly on the surface of the fabric — don't pull them taut or allow the ribbon to twist. Hold a needle or a finger of your non-working hand under the ribbon as you pull it through the fabric to stop the ribbon twisting. Always work with short lengths of ribbon as it is easily damaged. If you enjoy ribbon embroidery, you will be able to use it everywhere in crazy patchwork. If this is a new technique for you, refer to *Useful books* on page 70.

Beads

Always add these last, when all the embroidery is completed, otherwise your working threads will continually wrap around and catch on them. Beads of all shapes and sizes can be used to add spark to the embroidery, or can be used together to build up beadwork patterns.

Stitch beads to the surface of your work with a backstitch. The stitch should be exactly the size of the width of the bead, as this will help it stand up straight, and you will see shiny surfaces instead of lots of little doughnuts on your work. Take care not to pull the thread tight between each bead or your work will pucker. As you pull the thread through after attaching each bead, give it a little tug to help the bead stand up. If the beads insist on falling over, sometimes an extra stitch will make them more stable.

Do a couple of double stitches on the back of the work after every few beads, so that if one becomes detached, all the others in the row won't roll away with it. As you come close to the final stitching line at the edge of the patchwork, it is a

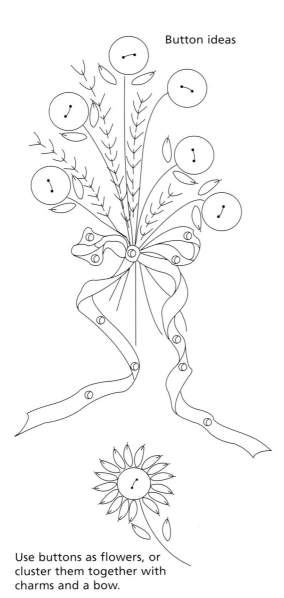

Button ideas

Use buttons as flowers, or cluster them together with charms and a bow.

good idea to secure each bead with a double stitch on the back of the work: then, if you need to, you will be able to remove any beads that get in the way of the sewing machine needle without losing the whole row.

Use beading thread and sharps or milliner's needles to attach beads.

Buttons, charms and other extras

Buttons and all sorts of treasures add an extra dimension to crazy patchwork. Like beads, they should be added last, even if you plan where to put them as you work, so that they don't catch threads while you are still doing the embroidery.

Little mother-of-pearl or shell buttons can be turned into flowers or flower centres (see page 66). Attach buttons with decorative thread if the thread will be visible.

Charms coloured gold and silver, and in shell and mother-of-pearl, are also available in a wide variety of shapes and sizes.

Mill Hill Treasures offer decorative shapes from hearts and flowers to Christmas trees. They can give a decorative touch, or add to the theme of your decoration. Attach them with a double stitch in beading thread or embroidery thread, or use decorative stitches, such as detached chain and long straight stitches.

Pins and needles

If you are going to do a lot of work with silks, lace and other fine fabrics, invest in a packet of brass silk pins. Many fine fabrics will retain the marks left by large pins, so it's important to use the finest pins you can get. And never leave pins or needles in fabric, even if you think it will be for only a short time — you don't always finish a piece when you plan to, and months later may find ugly rust marks in your work (and always in the most obvious spot). If you have ignored this advice, you can always hide a mark under a motif or a button.

Each project in this book lists the needles you need, depending on suggestions for embellishment. For general hand sewing, use a crewel or sharps needle — experiment to find one that suits you. For general sewing with machine cotton, use the finest needle you can cope with, or the finest you can thread — the higher the needle number, the finer it will be.

Always consider the thickness of the thread — it must pass easily through the eye of the needle — and the needle has to make a hole in the fabric large enough for the thread to pass through easily. If the eye of the needle damages the thread, choose a larger needle size. If you find yourself tugging needle and thread through the fabric, the needle is too small, so choose a larger one. This doesn't mean you should use the largest needle in the pack every time. If the needle is too large it will damage the fabric, and a smaller, finer needle is usually easier to sew with.

Crewel needles can be used for nearly all embroidery likely to be used in crazy patchwork. Size 9 or 10 can be used with one or two strands of stranded silk of cotton thread. Size 8 can be used with several strands of stranded silk or cotton, fine perle or soft cotton threads, such as the flower threads. Larger sizes, such as 5 and 3, can be used with thicker yarns. Mixed packets include sizes 3–10. Use crewel needles for buttonhole appliqué with paper-backed fusible web. Using the finest needle you can cope with is important, as the finer and sharper the needle, the easier it is to pierce the fabrics, which become firmer when web is used.

Chenille needles are much larger, and have much larger eyes. Mixed packets generally contain sizes 18–24, with size 18 the largest. Use chenille needles for ribbon embroidery and for sewing with thicker threads, such as chenille, or taking thick or fancy threads that have been couched through to the back of the work.

Straw or milliner's needles are good for working bullion stitch; choose larger sizes for more strands of thread or thick threads. Fine milliner's needles are also the best choice for working with metal threads. If you can get the very fine ones, in sizes 10–12, they are also good for beading and perfect for hand appliqué. Mixed packets are generally in sizes 5–10.

Betweens needles are used for hand quilting, and many quilters use them for hand piecing too. Use anything from size 8 to 12, depending on what you can thread and what feels most comfortable to use; the finer the needle the better.

Sharps needles are used for hand appliqué, and the fine ones are also good for beading too. These extend to fine number 12s; the finer the needle the better for making tiny stitches.

Beading needles are also available, but they are very long and very fragile, and they will be needed only for the most minute of beads. Fine sharps and milliner's needles can both be used for beading.

Twisted cords

Twisted cords make decorative edges for pieces such as the pincushion and scissor case in *The deep blue sea* projects (pages 35–42). They can be made in any thread, but number 5 perle cotton is a good choice. Cut a 15 cm piece of the yarn first to tie off the end when the cord is finished. Cut six lengths of cotton measuring three times the length of the final cord. Knot them together at one end, and put this over a hook or a doorknob. Standing at full distance from the hook, twist the threads until they start to kink. While holding the threads taut, place the index finger of your other hand at the centre point of the threads and bring the two ends together, so that the threads twist around each other. Use your free hand to smooth the twist. Tie the threads close to the end, and remove them from the hook.

Piping

Fabric-covered piping is used to finish the bag in *Out of this world* (pages 43–8). It is also useful for projects such as cushions. The project instructions describe how much piping to make, what cord to use, and how wide to cut the bias strips of fabric.

Cut bias strips from the project fabric in the width specified in the project, and join them together to form a strip of the specified length. Fold this strip over the piping cord, matching the raw edges, and pinning close to the piping. Take care not to twist the fabric as you work.

Using a longer-than-usual stitch on the sewing machine, stitch along the bias strip, close to the cord. A zipper foot lets you stitch close to the piping, but don't get as close to the piping as possible at this stage: this row of stitching should be a *little* further away so that it will be concealed when the piping is applied to the project.

To attach the piping, pin it to the right side of the project piece, matching the raw edges. Clip the binding a little on any curves and ease it round, so that it will not be tight when the project is complete. Using the zipper foot, attach the piping to the project piece, using the standard stitch size and stitching as closely to the piping as possible, to hide the first row of stitching in the seam allowance. Leave extra piping at the start and finish to turn to the wrong side, or overlap them in an unobtrusive place, taking them into the seam allowance.

Mitring

To mitre the corners for borders Attach one of the border strips to one side of the patchwork centre, with equal amounts of fabric at each end, starting and ending exactly 1 cm from each end. Stitch a second strip to an adjacent side in the same way.

Turn both strips to the right side, and press the seams. Where the two strips meet, lay one end of the fabric over the other, and fold it back at a 45 degree angle, carefully aligning the straight edges of the strips (see diagram), and pin. Press the fold.

Mitred corner for border

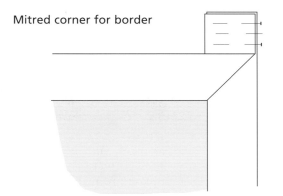

Folding the patchwork on the diagonal, and taking care not to shift the fabrics, stitch the two strips together along the fold, from the inner corner to the edge, and make some stitches a little beyond the edge. Feed the fabric carefully into the machine to avoid stretching along the bias line. Open out the mitre and check that it is lying flat and smooth. Trim the seam allowances to 5 mm and press them open. Repeat for each corner.

To mitre the corners for binding Start attaching the binding at least a third of the way along one edge. Stitch to exactly 1 cm from the corner of the next edge.

Fold the binding away from the quilt edge at a 45 degree angle (top diagram), then fold it down along the second edge, aligning the fold with the top edge (bottom diagram).

Mitred corner for binding

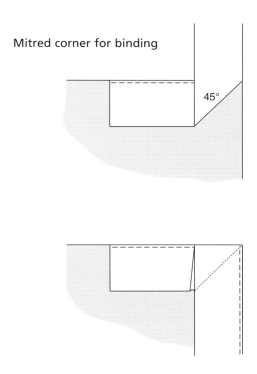

Start stitching again exactly 1 cm from the edge — do not stitch through the fold or the seam allowance. When you turn the binding to the back, the mitre will form on the front and you will be able to match it on the back.

Useful books

History of crazy patchwork

Fox, Sandi. *Wrapped in Glory: Figurative Quilts and Bedcovers, 1700–1900*. Thames & Hudson, London, 1990.

McMorris, Penny. *Crazy Quilts*. E. P. Dutton, New York, 1984.

Rolfe, Margaret. *Patchwork Quilts in Australia*. Greenhouse Publications, Richmond, Vic., 1987.

Rolfe, Margaret, and Moore, Val. *Patchwork, Appliqué and Quilting*. In Australian Heritage Needlework series (edited by Jennifer Sanders), Lothian, Port Melbourne, 1993 (methods and projects included).

Crazy patchwork methods

Montano, Judith. *The Crazy Quilt Handbook*. C&T Publishing, Lafayette, California, 1986.

Thomason, Lezette. *Victorian Elegance*. That Patchwork Place, Bothell, Washington, 1996.

Stitch books

Bond, Dorothy. *Crazy Quilt Stitches*. Self-published, Eugene Oregon, n.d.

Christie, Mrs Archibald. *Samplers and Stitches*. Batsford, London, 1st edn 1920, 5th edn published in paperback 1985.

Enthoven, Jacqueline. *The Stitches of Creative Embroidery*. Schiffer Publishing Co., West Chester, Pennsylvania, 1987.

Joynes, Heather. *Stitches for Embroidery*. Kangaroo Press, Kenthurst, NSW, 1991.

Nichols, Marion. *Encyclopedia of Embroidery Stitches, Including Crewel*. Dover Publications, New York, 1974.

Thomas, Mary. *Mary Thomas's Dictionary of Embroidery Stitches*. Hodder & Stoughton, London, first edn 1934 (reprinted many times, and now available in an updated version with colour diagrams).

Beadwork

Campbell-Harding, Valerie, and Watts, Pamela. *Bead Embroidery*. B. T. Batsford, London, 1993.

Thompson, Angela. *Embroidery with Beads*. B. T. Batsford, London, 1987.

Motifs

Lampe, Diana, with Fiske, Jane. *Embroidered Garden Flowers*. Sally Milner Publishing, Birchgrove, NSW, 1991.

Lampe, Diana. *More Embroidered Garden Flowers*. Sally Milner Publishing, Birchgrove, NSW, 1993.

Lawther, Gail. *Patterns and Borders Needlecraft Source Book*. Anaya Publishers, London, 1992.

Mostaghimi, Lynette. *Countryside Needlecraft Source Book*. Tiger Books International, London, 1994.

Tristram, Lindy. *Houses and Gardens Needlecraft Source Book*. Anaya Publishers, London, 1994.

Ribbon embroidery

Hiney, Mary Jo. *Victorian Ribbon and Lacecraft Designs*. Sterling Publishing Co., New York, 1993.

Joynes, Heather. *The Complete Book of Ribbon Embroidery*. Kangaroo Press, Kenthurst, NSW, 1992.

Joynes, Heather. *Old-fashioned Flowers in Ribbon and Threads*. Kangaroo Press, Kenthurst, NSW, 1994.

Macdonald, Robbyn. *Victorian Embroidery*. Sally Milner Publishing, Birchgrove, NSW, 1993.

Rankin, Chris. *Splendid Silk Ribbon Embroidery*. Sterling Publishing Co., New York, 1996.

Turpin-Delport, Lesley. *Just Flowers*. Triple T Publishing, Cape Town, 1994.

Suppliers

Most of the stores and sources listed supply by mail order. Try your local needlework specialist first, as staff can give invaluable advice. Craft shows allow you to buy from stores you can't normally visit or from show-only dealers.

Crazy patchwork classes

Ask at your local needlework, patchwork or craft store. The author teaches crazy patchwork at Ruth's Artneedle and Patchwork Plus in Sydney (contact information below).

Box kits

Helen Norton
PO Box 556, St Ives NSW 2075
Tel. 9983 9972
Produces the kit used for the rectangular box in *Peaches and cream,* and many other box kits. Phone for your nearest stockist or to obtain kits by mail order.

Fabrics

Lincraft
Bridal departments have a wonderful selection of fabrics suitable for crazy patchwork, and staff will happily sell you 10 cm strips (across the full width of the fabric). Stores also have embroidery thread (including silks), beads, patchwork fabrics and sewing supplies.

Patchwork Plus
7–15 Jackson Avenue, Miranda NSW 2228
Tel. (02) 9540 2780
Small cuts of silks and other fabrics suitable for crazy patchwork, patchwork fabrics, lace, embroidery threads (including silks), buttons and sewing supplies. Open seven days a week. Mail order. Crazy patchwork classes.

Japanese fabrics

Abundia
PO Box 282, Paddington QLD 4064
Tel./fax (07) 3367 2931
Antique and contemporary fabrics in silk and cotton, including traditional blue fabrics. Fabric club. Sells at craft shows. Mail order.

The Quilting Heart
10 Yallumba Close, Forestville NSW 2087
Tel./fax (02) 9452 2640
Antique and contemporary fabrics in silk and cotton, including traditional blue fabrics. Sells at craft shows. Mail order.

Sanshi
89a Palmerston Street, Mosman Park WA 6012
Tel. (09) 384 8244

Antique and contemporary fabrics in silk and cotton, including traditional blue fabrics. A range of Japanese threads. Sells at craft shows. Mail order.

Threads and ribbon

Cotton On Creations
PO Box 804, Epping NSW 2121
Tel. (02) 9868 4583
French laces, silk ribbons, YLI threads, Thread Packs. Wholesale only. Phone for nearest stockist.

DownUnder Australia
Retail store:
The Village Stitchery, 53 Ethel Street, Seaforth NSW 2092
Tel. (02) 9948 8750
Wholesale office:
Suite 3, 559 Sydney Road, Seaforth NSW 2092
Tel. (02) 9948 5575
Importers of Caron, Needle Necessities over-dyed threads, Leah's and Rainbow Gallery threads, Pètals silk ribbon. Phone wholesale office for nearest stockist.

Kacoonda threads
Box 6, Somers VIC 3927
Tel. (03) 5983 5506
Variegated threads in a variety of fibres and weights, and variegated silk ribbon. Wholesale only. Phone for nearest stockist.

Mosman Needlecraft
733 Military Road, Mosman
NSW 2088
Tel. (02) 9969 5105
Fax (02) 9969 5005
Threads, including variegated
standed cottons, full range
of Brazilian threads, Caron,
Rainbow Gallery, Au ver à
soie, Kacoonda threads; silk
ribbons, beads. Mail order.

Perri's Threads
PO Box 197, Canterbury
VIC 3126
Small mixed packets of
threads and ribbons, silk
threads. Sells at craft shows.
Mail order.

Ruth's Artneedle
Shop 12, Castle Plaza,
273 Old Northern Road,
Castle Hill NSW 2154
Tel. (02) 9634 5887

Silk ribbon, beads, basic
embroidery threads, Caron
threads, Petals ribbon, silk
ribbon, Gumnut threads,
buttons, beads, charms.
Mail order. Crazy patchwork
classes.

Stadia Trading
Retail store:
20 Elizabeth Street,
Paddington NSW 2021
Tel. (02) 9328 7900
Wholesale and mail order:
PO Box 357, Beaconsfield
NSW 2014
Tel. (02) 9565 4666;
Fax (02) 9565 4464
Basic embroidery threads,
Au ver à soie threads,
charms, buttons, Mill Hill
beads and treasures.
Mail order.

Elde Crafts
76 Main Street, Hahndorf
SA 5245
Tel. (08) 8388 7007
Amazing themed buttons, bows,
etc., ribbons, cotton laces. Sells
at craft shows. Mail order.

Judith & Kathryn
The Olde Barber Shoppe
69 Murray Street,
Tanunda SA 5352
Tel. (085) 633 404
Painted lace, ribbon roses, silk
pictures. Sells at craft shows.
Mail order.

Patchwork Supplies
43 Gloucester Street,
Highgate Hill QLD 4101
Tel. (07) 3844 9391
Fax (07) 3844 2392
Silk fabrics, ribbons, wonderful
embellishments, kits. Sells at
craft shows. Mail order.

Index